VOICES

of the

Vietnam War

TERRY L. NAU

First Stillwater River Publications Edition 2019.

Library of Congress Control Number:2019911295

ISBN-10: 1-950339-29-7
ISBN-13: 978-1-950339-29-7

1 2 3 4 5 6 7 8 9 10

Compiled and edited by Terry L. Nau
Published by Stillwater River Publications, Pawtucket, RI, USA.

Publisher's Cataloging-In-Publication Data
(Prepared by The Donohue Group, Inc.)

      Names: Nau, Terry L., compiler, editor.
      Title: Voices of the Vietnam War / [compiled and edited by] Terry L. Nau.
      Description: First Stillwater River Publications edition. | Pawtucket, RI, USA : Stillwater River Publications, 2019.
      Identifiers: ISBN 9781950339297 | ISBN 1950339297
      Subjects: LCSH: Vietnam War, 1961-1975--Personal narratives, American. | Vietnam War, 1961-1975--Veterans--United States. | Vietnam War, 1961-1975--Women--United States. | Military spouses--United States. | LCGFT: Personal narratives. | Oral histories.
      Classification: LCC DS559.5 .V65 2019 | DDC 959.7043092--dc23

ON THE COVER – Left: A female demonstrator offers a flower to military police on guard at the Pentagon during an anti-Vietnam demonstration. Arlington, Virginia, October 21, 1967. (National Archive); Center: David Christian visits his brother Doug's grave at Washington Crossing National Cemetery, not far from Dave's home. Doug died of cancer linked to Agent Orange exposure during the Vietnam War. (Photo courtesy of David Christian); Right: Members of Company C, 2nd Battalion, 35th Infantry, 3rd Brigade, 4th Infantry Division, move across an open field towards their objective during a search and destroy operation in the Quang Ngai Province, 22 miles northwest of their base camp at Duc Pho, October 25, 1967. (National Archive)

The views and opinions expressed in this book are solely those of the author and do not necessarily reflect the views and opinions of the publisher.

This book is dedicated to my Pennsbury High classmate, Edward McGurk, who died of Agent Orange-related cancer issues on May 29, 2019. This book is also dedicated to all of our Vietnam War veterans who have battled illnesses over the years that may have stemmed from their exposure to Agent Orange.

Table of Contents

PROLOGUE
The Untold Stories of War

BY TERRY NAU

After I retired from newspaper work in 2012, the urge to write about the Vietnam War came over me, and four books would follow over the next six years. Each book seemed to open a new path to undiscovered stories about the war. My first book was just a personal retelling of my own experience but the next three covered a wider expanse and after each of those books reached publication, someone would get in touch and tell me about a good story I had missed. I soon discovered a bunch of Pennsbury High School classmates and hometown friends who had fought in Vietnam, many more than I had realized. We had lost track of each other in those crazy days of the late-1960s.

This book is about some of those stories that escaped me. It begins with the tale of Army captain David A. Christian, one of the Vietnam War's most highly-decorated soldiers. Not sure how I missed this one. David's mother married my uncle, Tony Nau, in 1962, right around the time America was increasing its military commitment in Southeast Asia. I got drafted in 1966 and David, a year younger, signed up for the Army that same year at age 17. We did not know each other, growing up in adjoining Pennsylvania towns and attending high schools 10 miles apart.

David would become the youngest and most decorated officer in the Vietnam War. He was commissioned a 2nd Lt. before he turned 19 years old and went on medical retirement as a Captain three years later after sustaining severe burns and numerous other wounds while leading recon patrols for the 75th Rangers. His story has been told in an autobiography, *Victor Six*, but as David told me during interviews for this book, his original 500-page manuscript was cut in half by the publisher and its co-author, William Hoffer.

In this book, we focus on how David grew up poor in Levittown, went to work at age 13, and led an accelerated life that has barely slowed down over the years. David is now 71 years old, owns two companies, and travels extensively, often in support of fellow veterans.

There were other Vietnam veterans who would reveal themselves as my self-published books became available to friends and fellow veterans. These veterans became the voices of this book.

Terry Wallace, a 1964 graduate of Pennsbury High, got drafted in 1966 and was assigned to the Marine Corps, where he became a "tanker," not the safest infantry job you could find. Terry survived his 13 months of duty and left the war zone suffering from a concussion and some memory loss after his tank hit a mine. Wallace struggled in his first years at home but made his way through college and found work in the medical field. As the years went by, he began recording his experiences in a journal. I offered Terry a chance to put his work into this book. Terry responded by writing a wonderfully detailed account of his military experience. It is an honest appraisal of how the war impacted his life and quite interesting, too. This chapter proves my belief that every soldier has his own story to tell.

Until I began researching a book about my high school's 15 Vietnam War casualties, I had no idea that over 50 of my Class of 1965 colleagues had served their country in Vietnam. We had all traveled different paths as the draft honed in on us. College, marriage, military … those were the three main choices. Many young men caught in the crosshairs joined one of the other military branches in order to gain some control over their choice. The clearheaded youths who had connections or good timing joined the reserves. Six months active duty, six years of reserves. That seemed a long time to wear the uniform. The single tolerable dimension of the draft was the Army could keep draftees on active duty for just two years. The other military branches required at least three years of active duty. Many of us just rolled the dice and accepted the draft because it provided the quickest way home. The government responded by taking out a $10,000 insurance policy on soldiers, to be paid to next of kin in the event of death. At least soldiers now knew how much their lives were valued by the politicians.

Back in the 1960s, local draft boards held tremendous power over the lives of males between the ages of 18 and 26. Off-limits were the medically unfit, young fathers and college students. That covered about half the eligible soldier candidates. Among my high school classmates, Uncle Sam got us either in 1966 at age 19 or in 1969 after the college guys graduated. Or maybe when they dropped out of college, as happened to Don Bentivoglio, who joined the Army and became an infantry officer in 1969. More than half of the 350 males in my high school class ended up in the military by the early 1970s. About one in seven served in the Vietnam War. (The national average was one in 10.)

This book includes stories from where I grew up in Pennsylvania, and where I have lived the second half of my life – in Pawtucket, R.I. There are stories from Lower Bucks County that did not come to me in time for my book about Pennsbury High. Like the Little League World Championship baseball team from Levittown American that sent three players to Vietnam. One of them, Jimmy Grauel, went from the green, green grass of Williamsport to the rice paddies of Vietnam in six short years.

As I began putting this book together, a Vietnam veteran from my Class of 1965, Ed McGurk, endured a difficult surgery for throat cancer, fighting each day to stay alive and come home to his family. Eddie was perhaps the most popular person in our class of 725 students. He was a big kid who played football and wrestled. Our yearbook is filled with photos of Eddie smiling while interacting with fellow students. A few years later, he would be fighting a grim war 10,000 miles from home. Ed was sprayed with the dioxin known as Agent Orange and developed health issues related to that poison as he reached his 60s. The Veterans Administration granted him disability compensation for Agent Orange-linked diseases, such as cancer.

Eddie told me during our 50th reunion, "They're just paying me to die." The smile was still there, just not as big, and a bit forced. He died on May 29, 2019 at the age of 71. The line for his funeral snaked outside the Beck-Dougherty Funeral Home. This book is dedicated to Ed, and all the other Vietnam veterans who have died from or live with diseases linked to Agent Orange.

There were also stories that developed after I wrote about the 21 KIA from my adopted hometown of Pawtucket, where I have lived since 1982. The biggest story tells how the people of Pawtucket never forgot those 21 Heroes. They helped raise $40,000 for a monument that honored all 21 of those soldiers. We installed that monument in 2017 in a beautiful part of the local park. It has become a place where people come to sit on a bench and reflect upon those 21 shortened lives. That saga is another chapter in this book.

We have a chapter written by Stephen Walach, a Pawtucket resident, who grew up with two of the 21 Heroes – Bobby Taylor and Michael Dalton. Steve received Conscientious Objector's status not long before Michael Dalton died and explains his thinking during this complicated chapter that shines a light on the terrible choices thrust upon Baby Boomers during the Vietnam War.

My Pawtucket golf buddy, Jim Raftus, has contributed a chapter about his service as a "reluctant" Army soldier who served the bulk of his time in Alaska, the closest place in America to the Soviet Union. Jim could not see Russia from his military post but he did have an officer tell him the "Rooskies" would come right over the border and hit Alaska first if a new World War erupted.

Everyone who grew up in the mid-1960s was impacted by Vietnam. My high school classmate, Liza Hamill, shares her own story of protesting the war while in college. We are growing older together, the protestors and the veterans. Growing older and still learning about each other.

Later on in this book come successive chapters about two career Army officers, Wardell Hollis and Gary Perryman, who met in ROTC at Oklahoma State University and bounced into each other again in Vietnam. Their stories speak to the patriotism that is often overlooked in our recollections of the 1960s. Many young men and women did join the military with high aspirations, hoping to succeed in a disciplined profession. Vietnam tested our military's capabilities but never the abilities of its patriotic soldiers.

For the final chapter in this book, I interviewed a veteran who went back to Vietnam in 2018 to answer some of his lingering questions about the war. Dick Muth and his wife, Darlene, met a Vietnamese farmer named Say who showed them an old fire base, now mostly grown over, that Dick helped build in 1967. Say told Dick and Darlene how an abandoned minefield outside the base killed approximately 10 farmers over the years before it was finally neutralized in the early 1990s. Say remembered the fiery napalm attacks during the war, not assessing any blame because his family was loyal to the South Vietnamese and, by extension, the American soldiers who passed in their midst.

The farmer told Dick Muth, "We look to the future, not the past." Good advice for all of us.

NEW FRIENDS – Dick Muth and his wife Darlene shared a moment at the home of a Vietnamese farmer named Say and his family during a visit to Vietnam in 2018. (Photo courtesy of Dick Muth)

CHAPTER ONE
David Christian Never Stopped Fighting

BY TERRY NAU

David Christian has a quick answer when asked about his greatest achievement.

"My family," the Florida native said while sitting in the study of his home in Washington Crossing, Pa. during the spring of 2019. The backyard of his colonial style home, purchased in 1977, abuts the Delaware Canal. Just beyond the canal is the Delaware River, not far from where General Washington and his troops crossed over to fight the Battle of Trenton in 1776. Dave and Peggy Christian raised their four children in this house and seem comfortable here as they grow older. One of their grandsons is working out back as the old soldier reminisces about his days as an infantry officer in the Vietnam War.

"Peggy and I have three daughters and a son," Christian pointed out. "They all graduated from Villanova University. That's where I got my undergraduate degree. We are a Villanova family."

Just moments earlier, a blond-haired teenager had finished working around the back of the house.

"My grandson was here this morning, painting a fence for us. His name is Jay Burke. Jay just celebrated his 19th birthday."

Christian looked at his interviewer and smiled.

"When I was 18, I was considered the youngest officer in the Army, and when I was 19 I was leading a recon platoon in Vietnam. I would sit down in meetings with colonels and majors, providing information so they could make decisions. I was the youngest commissioned officer in the Army since the Civil War."

A lot of people still blink twice when they hear David Christian's story of being a teenage combat officer in Vietnam. The story makes more sense once you hear how David's life sped by so quickly as a child.

"I grew up a lot different than you did," Christian said. "My father (M.J. Christian) left our family when I was seven. My mother, Dorothy Christian, was the sole source of support when we were little. I became the man of the house, trying to take care of things for my mom. In those days, the state did not give out food stamps. Families in need waited in line for surplus food. We would go over to Bristol and stand in line. Other kids would see us in what were called the 'poor lines' and they would tease us at school.

"My mother was a very strong woman, even though she stood only 4 feet, 11 inches tall," Christian added. "She joined the Women's Army Corp (WAC). She worked on General (Douglas) MacArthur's staff, writing and typing up press releases. She was with the General in the Philippines, and went with him to Australia. She met my father during this period. He was a typewriter repairman. MacArthur loved his publicity and probably considered fixing a typewriter more important than fixing a jeep. My parents married after the war. My dad had a drinking problem and it got worse. They originally lived in Gainesville, FL., where the Christian family owned 500 acres of land, but my mom eventually decided it might be best to move back to her hometown, Croydon, not far from Philadelphia. Dad was in heaven when he got there because there was a bar on almost every street corner. One day, he went off to get the lawn mower fixed and never came home."

There were four children in the family – Douglas, David, Daniel and Dorothea. They were very close to each other, latch-key kids before the term became popular. David would do anything to help his mother. When he was 13, he hitchhiked to New York City, hoping to find work and send money home to help pay the mortgage.

"I had done a lot of reading as a kid, after everyone went to bed," Christian said. "New York City fascinated me. I would see shows on television that were set in New York. It wasn't more than 90 miles away from us. Back then, hitchhiking was pretty common. Kids were hitching all over the place. Some cars still had running boards. A kid could hop on the side of the car and get a lift that way. With my mother's permission, I set off for New York. I ended up in Manhattan, asking for jobs, but nobody would hire me. I went over to Brooklyn. Same thing. I lied about my age, told them I was 15 or 16, even 17. I rubbed the powder from concrete on my face to cover up my peach fuzz. Finally, one day I walked into a place in Brooklyn. The guy said he would hire me but if anyone asked, I should say I was part of their family. That was because unions were so strong in those days. This was 1961. If you don't say you are family, you get the owners in trouble. I got work as a carpenter's helper, at Flatbush and Atlantic Avenue. I worked as a laborer, hauling 2 x 4s back and forth, doing anything I could. I lived in the bowling alley that we were tearing out. I still remember the name of those alleys – State Lanes. The construction company also had a little hotel nearby where the crew could rent rooms for $15 a week. Just a small room. And a communal shower.

"The streets were tough. You walk to the wrong corner and all of a sudden you were in a confrontation. Every gang of kids had their own turf. The workers would head to the bar after our shift ended. Sometimes I would go with them and get served. I got paid $1.50 an hour, pretty good money in 1961. I worked a lot of hours. Kept $15 for subsistence and sent the rest home to my mother. Our mortgage was $83 a month. That wasn't a big mortgage but when you have no money, it's like a million dollars."

After four months, David returned home to Levittown and resumed school. He spent one year at Bishop Egan High School, where he first met his future wife, Peggy Todd, and finished up at Woodrow Wilson, where he graduated with honors. That's the linear version of his story. The real life version was more complicated.

"In our family, when you turned 16, you were on your own," Christian recalled. "You had to get a job. I turned 16 in 12th grade. I asked my mother if I could stay in high school and graduate. She said if you get a job and make a man's wage, you can stay in school. I got a job in Tullytown, at a place called Optical Scanning. I became the foreman's supervisor on the night shift. Working when I was 13 had given me a lot of confidence in myself. I learned that I had to push myself on people. The answer would always be no unless you asked. I got that from my mother. Mom always had to fight for things. She taught me it doesn't matter what size you are. Speak up. You have to have a voice,

3

and assert yourself. All through my life, I have spoken out against things that I thought were wrong."

Long story short, David Christian graduated from Woodrow Wilson High in 1966, at the age of 17, and he was in a hurry to get going with the next stage of his life. Dave and his mother talked about how the GI Bill would pay for his college, if he first joined the military and put in his time. The family's military tradition also played a role. Dave's great-grandfather on his father's side had fought for the Confederacy just over 100 years earlier. The Vietnam War was heating up in 1966.

"I joined the Army right away," he said. "In basic training, I figured I was smarter than my drill sergeants. I wanted to be a leader myself, an officer. I had read in the *Army Times* that the Army was really afraid of Congress."

Pushing forward, as always, David Christian wrote and mailed a letter to the Congressional Armed Services Committee, asking for the opportunity to attend Officer's Candidate School despite his age. The Army preferred its officer candidates to be at least 19 years old.

"The letter got passed around and then back to my commanding officer," Christian recalled. "The issue was whether I would be allowed to take the test for Officer's Candidate School at the age of 17. My unit commander said, 'You really have balls, kid. What are you doing? You are 17 and want to become an officer? That's too young!' I just told him I would like to take the test. I knew I was too young. The Army also decided I was too young but they had a compromise. They would give me an IQ test. I did so well on that test, they let me take the test for OCS. At this point, I was doing my basic training at Fort Gordon, GA. I graduated at the head of my class and got promoted to E-3. Then I went to advanced infantry training at Fort Ord, CA. Every time I graduated it was at the top of my class and I got promoted each time. I was a Corporal (E4) out in California and still only 17 years old (Christian's 18th birthday fell on Oct. 26, 1966). I remember going into an Enlisted Men's Club on the base. The guys inside challenged me almost right away. They thought I was too young to be in there. They said, 'Corporal Christian, let us see your ID card.' My card proved that

I could wear the corporal's stripes. I liked hearing 'Corporal Christian.' I wrote a letter home to my mother and signed it, 'Corporal Christian.'

"Not too much later, I got called into my commanding officer's office, which was called the CQ. He says to me, 'Who do you know in Washington? We have orders for you to go to Officer's Candidate School. Who do you know?' I just told him my story of how I asked to take the test. I think this was an Army snafu. I was supposed to wait until I was 19 but the orders came ahead of time."

Christian arrived at OCS and immediately began proving himself as a soldier and a person who could get things done.

"At OCS, nobody ever asked me my age. In addition to the training, I kept myself busy doing odd jobs. They needed a court martial room built. Who could read blueprints? I said I could. I had carpenter skills, too. I started doing jobs, built a couple of things, customized some rooms, put closets in them, that kind of stuff. Nobody really questioned my age because I kept so busy. The day before I was supposed to graduate, the training officer called me in. I thought something was up. The Lieutenant asks me, 'How old are you?' I'm 18, sir. The Lieutenant says, 'Oh my God, how did this happen? How did you get here?' I told him my story. He starts telling me I am going to be leading men into battle who are all older than me. Some of them are NCOs who have children older than me. He says, 'Whatever you do, do not tell them your age. When somebody asks, just change the subject. Don't ever lie to anyone. Just change the subject. That was really good advice."

Christian graduated from OCS on Aug. 1, 1967. His mother and younger brother Daniel came down for the ceremony. According to David's autobiography, *Victor Six,* "Dot Christian pinned the Lieutenant bars on her second son, beamed and said, 'I would like to burst.' At the age of 18, her son was the youngest officer in the United States Army."

The bold young officer would spend the next six months polishing his combat skills. He went to Airborne School and then to the JFK Special Welfare Center. He earned his Special Forces patch and became a Green Beret. Still only 18 years old.

During this time, David was stationed at Fort Bragg, N.C. So was his brother Doug, an enlisted man back in the states between tours of Vietnam. The two siblings would sometimes venture nine hours north by car to their mom's home in Levittown. Dave pursued his relationship with Peggy Todd. They would be married before David left for Vietnam in the late spring of 1968.

Sadly, Dorothy Christian died at home on the night of Jan. 21, 1968, after suffering from pneumonia. David and Doug Christian left Fort Bragg without official permission to attend their mother's funeral. Doug received an Article 15 for going AWOL, absent without leave, while David was reprimanded and warned he might have to repeat his training. David could hardly hear through his grief, according to his recollection in *Victor Six*.

"You're getting things out of priority," a Lieutenant Colonel told Dave. "People are going to die. You have to get used to that. The Army is your family now."

In the spring of 1968, David Christian married Peggy, completed his training, and left for the Republic of Vietnam (RVN), where he was assigned to the First Infantry Division, 75th Rangers. Christian soon became Executive Officer of a Long Range Reconnaissance Patrol outfit, the "LRRPs," as they were known. These were small teams of soldiers, between five and a dozen, who would go out on missions, looking for the enemy and collecting intelligence.

Lt. Christian proved to be a quick study. He earned the respect of his soldiers at a time in the war when the American commitment at the highest levels was being called into question by soldiers who were fighting and dying in RVN. It was not uncommon for American combat troops to opt for discretion over valor. And if an officer proved too careless with his soldiers' lives, he might end up on the wrong end of a "fragging" incident.

"Over 200 officers were reported to have been fragged in Vietnam," Christian told the author in a final interview for this book in June 2019. "This often came down to an officer not knowing how to do his job."

That was never a question for Lt. Christian, who would convince his recon patrol team that seeking out and killing the enemy was safer than laying back in the jungle and fighting passively. Over the next few months, Christian and his soldiers would discover 52 enemy camps. His men truly believed they "owned the jungle."

"Dave came to recon a few months after I arrived," recalled Jim Lowe, one of Christian's troops, in a *YouTube* interview. "I knew he was a lot younger than me. I was 23 at the time. We had a lot of Lieutenants who were greenhorns. Dave came in and not only knew how to read a map, he never got lost. He always knew our objective. Dave was a true leader. Because Dave could read a map and knew exactly where he was, he could call in mortars, sometimes within 10 meters of the target. His abilities amazed all of us. He trained us to be leaders, too. He taught us how to read maps. We had a lot of good soldiers and Dave knew how to bring out (the best) in us."

Lowe and his fellow recon members never questioned Lt. Christian's leadership skills, not after the first few days, and did not regard his youthfulness as an important issue. This new officer looked pretty young but he wanted to lead them and his tactics might save their lives. Those were the two most important qualities infantry soldiers wanted to see in their officers.

"Dave loved being an officer and he worked hard at it," Lowe said. "He was diligent. Some of the other officers we had were just serving their time, like a lot of the soldiers. Dave wasn't that way. He wanted to be a leader and he was the best at it."

Christian's idea of combat revolved around one concept: be aggressive. After about one month in the war zone, Christian's fighting plan had evolved, with help from his own soldiers, and through close observance of the enemy's hit-and-run tactics. He took all of his stateside training and applied it to the problems he was now encountering in the jungle.

"When firefights broke out, both sides would get really quiet after the initial contact was made," Christian explained. "I remember watching old movies where the Indians would come out screaming when they attacked. I told my guys that's what we needed to do when we were within the crosshairs of the enemy. Soldiers want to hug the ground when a firefight starts. My job as an officer was to tell them to stand up and charge, screaming like banshees, or rebels. Oh, we had our rebel yells. We had quite a few southern soldiers in our unit. One guy from Louisiana grew up hunting in the woods and when he went home he went back to the woods. You don't really think about the environment of war until you are immersed in it. And then you have to react. If you hug the ground, the enemy is going to bring in reinforcements, he's going to zero in his weapons on your position, and you are going to die. My plan was always to get up and attack."

One incident described in *Victor Six* sort of says it all about the 19-year-old Lieutenant. His patrol was out in the jungle, searching for an enemy base without much luck, and being harassed by occasional gunfire, which Christian soon realized came from a couple of teenage enemy soldiers – VC, as the Americans called them. Dave hated their hit-and-run tactics. After twice dodging bullets, Lt. Christian took off running in the direction of the gunfire and chased the stunned teenagers down.

"You little bastards! I've had it with you," Christian wrote in his book, recalling the anger that flared up as he ran the two scrawny enemy down, tackling and disarming them. Christian wrote that he yelled at them, "Fight like men! Damn it, if you're going to fight, fight like men!" The two teenagers lay dazed and whimpering, waiting wide-eyed for certain death, according to *Victor Six*. They were no more stunned then Christian's recon team, which had seen their leader drop his M16 and charge after the enemy with little regard for his own life. Their belief in this new Lieutenant began to build rapidly from that day on.

Over the next few months, Christian's recon teams would out-shine other units in the First Infantry Division, drawing attention and some skepticism over their casualty reports. "Division scuttlebutt held that Christian was either incredibly savvy or incredibly luck," *Victor Six* reported in his autobiography.

On one mission, Christian's "Lurps" killed three NVA soldiers during an attack on an enemy outpost. When Christian reported the body count over the unit's radio network, he was greeted with these words: "Oh, sure." That set Lt. Christian off. He ordered his men to pick up the three dead NVA and take them back on the helicopter that would return them to base camp.

CHRISTIAN'S BUTCHERS – Members of the 75th Rangers Long Range Recon Patrol gather around Lt. David Christian (center right in floppy hat) during a break from action. (Photo courtesy of David Christian)

Back at camp, the patrol loaded the bodies on the back of a truck. Christian took the wheel and dumped the bodies outside the Division Tactical Operations Center. That pissed off everyone inside the bunker except for a Lt. Colonel who decided this brash young officer might be a valuable asset.

"Every once in a while, I run across someone who has a sixth sense for combat," the LTC said, as reported in *Victor Six*. Lt. Christian's role would expand in this war as the enemy began to build up its troop strength along the nearby Cambodian border.

Christian's unit would self-name itself, *"Christian's Butchers."* As the summer advanced, their recon patrols netted more enemy kills and brought back significant intelligence taken from the dead, including valuable maps. The Butchers' mission was to serve as a scout unit for the 1/26 Infantry. They also worked with the 11th Armored Cavalry Division, headed by Col. George S. Patton, Jr. By the end of October, they would have humped through missions all over War Zone C, earning a reputation as one of the best recon units in the Army.

The patrol's nickname seemed crude to outsiders, even in a war zone, but recon soldiers fought with honor.

"(*Christian's Butchers*) just materialized," said team member Tom Milam, many years later in a *YouTube* interview. "That was our nickname. I am very, very proud of recon. War is pure hell. To be involved with a unit like this, a special operations unit, have the success we had, with as few casualties as we had, that's a major accomplishment. Our mission was to find the enemy, which we did with great success."

Members of Christian's squad included Lowe and Milam, Dennis Going, Sam Janney, Staff Sergeant Woodruff, Gunnar Pawlata, James Scott, Jesse Lascano, Pete Andrews, Adam Gonzalez and Max Marinelli.

By late July, David Christian was promoted to 1st Lt. He was three months shy of his 20th birthday. By now, the age question had been completely forgotten. This brash young officer had won over his own men, and earned the grudging respect of fellow officers.

In late October, Christian's unit, fighting near the "Parrot's Beak" portion of the Cambodian border, launched an operation from Fire Support Base Rita and soon encountered a much larger force of NVA. A major firefight ensued, with *Christian's Butchers* unloading their weapons in a quick burst before their Lieutenant ordered them to bring out their LAWs, an anti-tank weapon. Knowing he was outnumbered by the enemy, Christian planned to simulate an artillery attack with the LAWs, his soldiers firing these heavy weapons in a one-two fashion. That would discourage the enemy from attacking his small force. The NVA did indeed fall for the ruse and depart the scene. Christian calmly called in an artillery barrage of white phosphorous shells, the worst kind of aerial news for the enemy.

On Oct. 29, 1968, just three days after his 20th birthday, 1st Lt. Christian and his men encountered another strong NVA force inside the Cambodian border. This time, there was no solution, no easy way out. The Butchers were pinned down. The enemy bought time in order to bring in more troops. Christian got on the radio to call in artillery. Two of his soldiers were wounded by light machine gun fire. Locating the machine gun bunker, Christian took out a grenade and charged, perfectly timing his deposit of the grenade into the bunker. After the explosion, Christian looked up to see an enemy soldier with an AK47 pointing at his face. A click was heard. The gun had jammed! Christian grabbed the enemy around his neck, began a death struggle, only to see him escape off into the jungle after Christian was distracted by noise coming from his men, who were cheering him on.

Christian, fueled by an adrenalin only hand-to-hand fighting can bring, looked back at his men and yelled, "What is the spirit of the bayonet?" They yelled back, "To kill!!!" Old training lessons are never forgotten.

Another machine gun began penetrating the Butchers' position in the jungle. Lt. Christian asked for two volunteers and went after this bunker. When they got close, Christian unleashed his LAW and blew up the bunker. However, a burst of enemy fire ripped into the tube of Christian's other LAW, sending shrapnel through his right hand. Within minutes, medic James Scott had arrived to wrap a field dressing around the wound. Scotty then crawled back to the rest of the patrol, but he was hit by enemy fire.

James Scott died in Lt. Christian's arms, as David pleaded for him to hang on. This was the first casualty in the nearly five months that he had been leading Recon. Several other troops had been wounded. Recon was running out of ammo. Gunnar Pawlata, with only a flare left in his arsenal, fired towards a bunker and hit an enemy soldier in the face. Christian got on the battalion radio network and called in artillery close to his position. Within minutes, shells were pounding the perimeter, chewing up enemy soldiers. Artillery support could be the infantry's best friend and 1st Lt. Christian, with his ability to read maps precisely, had used the big guns to end this battle.

Not long after, a squad from Delta Company arrived to help police the site and retrieve enemy intelligence. As David Christian sifted through the dead bodies, he passed over one enemy with a leg blown off. Christian searched him quickly for maps and suddenly felt a heartbeat. The young officer succumbed to a moment of compassion and decided to let the enemy soldier live. As he turned away, the enemy sprung up and stabbed Christian in his right arm with a knife, initiating a violent struggle that lasted for a couple of minutes until the American finished strangling his opponent to death. It was kill or be killed.

Once the Recon patrol got back inside the border of Vietnam, carrying its dead medic, James Scott, on a stretcher, a helicopter landed and returned the men to base camp. It was a somber ride, full of anger and sadness. Recon had lost its first soldier. As David Christian wrote in his book, they were no longer invulnerable.

Christian and several other members of recon received medical attention for their wounds. A priest, seeing Christian's bloodied body, actually performed Last Rites on the officer, prematurely as it turned out.

Many years later, in the spring of 2019, David Christian would sit in his home and reflect on those days of war. He is a thoughtful man who has pondered the subject of combat for more than 50 years. He seems to have examined all sides of war.

"What is courage?" he asked, repeating a question posed to him. "To me, courage is just getting your job done and bringing your men back alive. Courage is not defined in your heart. It is defined by your men, and by your superior officers. If you are defining your own courage, you are misinformed. I had self-doubts as a soldier, like everyone else. I remember reading about Joe Louis and Muhammad Ali, two great boxers, and General Patton. They all stated if you are going into a conflict, or into a fight, if you don't have caution, which could be interpreted as a degree of fear, then you are a fool. All of my missions in Vietnam, we had a degree of caution. But when you are between the ages of 18 and I would say, 27, you think you are invincible. When you have that philosophy at a young age, when they send you into battle and you have some success, that young GI becomes more confident in his invincibility ... until he holds a dying man in his arms."

1ˢᵗ Lt. Christian ended up at the 24ᵗʰ Evac Hospital in Long Binh, just outside of Saigon, where doctors examined his right hand. The ulnar nerve had been severed by the enemy soldier's knife. Permanent paralysis was a possibility discussed at the time. In addition, Christian had shrapnel fragments throughout the lower abdomen, a knife laceration in his right arm, and a deep wound in the upper back. According to *Victor Six*, "By the time they finished counting, medics found more than 100 holes in Christian's body."

The right hand injury concerned doctors the most. Christian remained in bed, his right arm elevated, worried about how he would go through life with a paralyzed hand. Any surgery would have to be performed at Camp Zama, a hospital in Tokyo. Before he left, doctors determined Christian was also afflicted with a serious parasitic infection.

There was plenty of time to contemplate his future in Japan. Word surfaced that Christian had twice been nominated for the Congressional Medal of Honor for his recent actions in Cambodia and Parrot's Beak. Recon had been assigned a new commander in his absence. The new leader retreated at the sound of first contact with the enemy. Christian's troops completed their mission on their own. He had trained them well.

A complicated surgery on his right hand followed, resulting in 120 suture wounds. Peggy, seven months pregnant, arrived in Tokyo to visit on Dec. 21, 1968. She wanted to talk her husband out of returning to the war when his wounds healed. They spent nearly two weeks together in Tokyo and when Peggy left, 1ˢᵗ Lt. Christian returned to the hospital, still without orders. By early January, he was in Saigon at the behest of the CIA, waiting for a special assignment that never materialized because the Army wanted to protect this young officer who was up for the Congressional Medal of Honor.

The highest medal would never come Christian's way but he did receive the next best, the Distinguished Service Cross, along with two Silver Stars for his actions between Sept. 23 and Oct. 29, 1968.

The DSC Citation reads, in part: "First Lt. Christian distinguished himself by exceptionally valorous actions on 29 October 1968 while in charge of the lead element of a reconnaissance-in-force mission ten miles northwest of Quan Loi. During an attempt to flank enemy positions, Lt. Christian's nine-man unit came under heavy rocket-propelled grenade, small arms and automatic weapons fire. After firing several light antitank weapons, he led an assault on the hostile strongholds, killing three North Vietnamese soldiers and causing others to flee. As he and his comrades advanced, they again received intense small arms and machine gun fire and three men were wounded. Lt. Christian sent the casualties and the medic to the rear and then led his troops forward until they became pinned down within ten meters of a bunker. Disregarding his safety, he assaulted the fortification single-handedly and destroyed it with hand grenades. The communists were reinforced by approximately thirty men, forcing the recon team to take cover behind a berm. Despite the enemy's devastating fire superiority, Lt. Christian attacked them with two antitank weapons. He was painfully wounded in the hand but refused medical care and returned to the berm to direct artillery fire.

"When friendly reinforcements arrived two hours later, he directed them to cover his left flank while he attempted to evacuate his casualties. Although wounded again by an enemy rocket-propelled grenade, he did not permit himself to be treated until the other injured men had been evacuated. Lt. Christian's extraordinary heroism and devotion to duty were in the highest traditions of the military service and reflect great honor on him, his unit and the United States Army."

After Peggy returned home from Japan, First Lt. Christian was assigned to the 18th MP Unit in Qui Nhon, on the shoreline of the South China Sea, not far from Hue. David Christian had been transferred out of his unit and he wasn't happy about it. But things happen quickly in a war zone and by late January, 1st Lt. Christian had been ordered back to his old stomping grounds at Lai Khe Base Camp. He reunited with some of his recon soldiers. Christian wanted to get his unit back together but was turned down by his new battalion commander, who sent him back to Qui Nhon for what appeared to be a stretch of rear-echelon duty that Christian had regarded with contempt all through his combat tour.

Fortunately for him, the enemy blew up an ammo dump at the camp and then shot up the Enlisted Men's Club! That was the final straw. Christian was called into the CQ's office and assigned to form a patrol that would locate the enemy's infiltration routes and burn them out with a canister of napalm.

This would be a tricky job. According to *Victor Six's* retelling, Christian's unit hauled a 50-gallon canister of napalm to the edge of a cliff that overlooked the enemy infiltration routes. Leading from the front, as always, Christian and a PFC named Tex (last name lost to time) carried buckets full of napalm down the slope of the cliff while others remained above, holding the canister in place. Christian and Tex spread the buckets of napalm along the elephant grass, moved off to one side, and ignited it. As they began to climb back up the slope, an explosion rocked the area. Christian believed a rocket-propelled grenade (RPG) or satchel charge caused the explosion. The enemy must have been spying on them. Still, this was a manageable situation until one of the American soldiers up above panicked and pushed the heavy canister of napalm down the hill, where it merged with the napalm that Tex and Christian had splashed into the elephant grass. Flames jumped 100 feet in the air and enveloped Christian and Tex.

"We heard the clicks (that ignited the explosion)," Christian said in a 2019 interview, thinking back on the napalm incident that resulted in 40 percent of his body suffering burns, including 24 percent third-degree burns that took all the skin away. "We saw enemy tracks, foot traffic in the grass. Then we heard the clicks. They must have set off the claymores. Me and Tex started running to the cliff. The rest of the platoon was up on top. Tex and I were hit by a blanket of flames that just swooped in on us, very suddenly. I tried to climb back up the cliff. I could feel the flames licking up under my pants, in the crotch area. I could hear Tex screaming. We couldn't see each other through the flames. I finally got on top of the cliff. Most of my clothes had been burned off my body. My jacket was gone. Flames were still coming up from my midsection. The guys came over and started rolling me on the ground to put out the fire."

A Sergeant came over and told Christian he had to go back down and get Tex. Christian figured they must think I am burned already. What's the harm?

"I went back towards the flames and saw this dark figure coming at me," Christian recalled in 2019. "It was on fire. This was Tex. He put his hands up and you could see his fingers were burned to the knuckles. I rolled him around on the ground to put the flames out. They choppered us back to Qui Nhon, to the 67th Evac. Doctors stabilized us."

This was the worst time of Christian's life. Within a few weeks, he found himself back in Japan, and the 106th General Hospital in Yokohama, fighting to stay alive in the burn ward. After his temperature dropped below 100 degrees on Feb. 11, David Christian was flown back to the states. Over the next six years, he would undergo 33 operations to repair his body from the traumatic burns. The war was over for David Christian. The Army would award him the Distinguished Service Cross for his extraordinary heroism on Oct. 29, 1968. Christian would also receive two Silver Stars and two Bronze Stars for valor. He would receive seven Purple Hearts that covered his various wounds from the war. More awards followed, beginning with the Republic of Vietnam Gallantry Cross with Star and Palm, the Legion of Merit, and the Army Commendation Medal. David Christian would become known as the most heavily decorated American soldier of the Vietnam War.

The Army medically retired Christian from active duty on July 4, 1970 as a Captain while he was undergoing treatment at Valley Forge Military Hospital, only 30 miles from home. He would see things in the burn wards that stayed with him forever, soldiers burned all over their bodies, dying in the night and wheeled away before other patients could notice they were gone.

"In the burn ward, they were taking two or three people away almost every night," Christian recalled. "We felt it was okay. They had fought the good fight and finally just gave up. In the burn ward, the Army had a rule. You could only take morphine for 72 hours and then they put you on Darvon. That was just too much pain for some of the guys. They were so crowded at Valley Forge, there were beds in the hallways. I saw tragedy everywhere. I wanted to fight for these guys and the only way I could do it was to help them fill out forms to get their disability benefits. As a Captain, I could do that. In the Army, you have to know what your mission is. My mission soon became these war veterans at Valley Forge."

As the 1970s began, David and Peggy Christian began raising their ever-growing family. At the same time, he enrolled at Villanova University and graduated just 19 months later, making the Dean's List during six of his eight semesters. Christian took advantage of the G.I. Bill to pay most of his college expenses, just as he and his mother had planned back in 1966.

The war would never leave David Christian alone, especially not in those early years after he came home. He was in and out of hospitals, undergoing numerous surgeries, mostly to repair the skin that had been lost in the napalm incident. After graduating from Villanova, he enrolled in Law School at Rutgers University, in New Brunswick, N.J.

Anti-war war sentiment still hung heavily around metropolitan colleges like Rutgers, and when a newspaper article appeared that detailed Christian's illustrious war record, the animosity for Vietnam veterans was directed at this most decorated of combat heroes. David Christian had reluctantly become a public figure because of the media attention his war record attracted.

Riding an elevator at Rutgers one day, Christian listened to a student ask him, "Did you meet the warmonger yet?" Christian answered back. "What warmonger – who's that?" The student said, "The guy that killed all those women and children and got a bunch of medals for it – a real creep."

David Christian, fighting on his own soil now, responded: "You're talking about me, and I never killed any women or children." (This anecdote appeared in a *People Magazine* article about Christian published in 1981.)

One professor called Christian into his office, asked him to take off his shirt, and then probed the young veteran's back, sticking a pencil into one of the deeper scars.

"I was asked by the administration to disrobe in front of the student body because they didn't think I was a disabled veteran. If I got a grade that was marginal, they would release it to the news media," Christian told the *Philadelphia Inquirer* in May 2011, as he returned to Rutgers to collect his long-delayed law degree from the school. Christian had dropped out of law school nearly 40 years earlier, in part because his still healing body could not sit in a chair for the six-hour long bar exam. He only needed eight credits to complete his degree.

In 2009, Christian's daughter Colleen contacted Rutgers to ask if her father could return to law school and finish what he had started four decades earlier.

"The new dean happened to be a Vietnam veteran, Rayman Solomon," Christian told *The Inquirer*. "He was shocked at this social tragedy."

Christian returned to school and graduated with his law degree in 2011 at the age of 62.

The chapters of David Christian's life after Vietnam are as full of action as his time in the war zone. He never stopped working to help his fellow veterans. Over a span of 40 years, he met every American President from Carter to Obama. He became a founding member of the Council on Vietnam Veterans and later the United Vietnam Veterans Organization (UVVO). He helped raise 10 million dollars to build the Vietnam Veterans Memorial in Washington, D.C. Behind that effort is a story that speaks to David Christian's importance in the Vietnam veteran community.

"(Wall founder) Jan Scruggs called me and said he was coming to Philadelphia for an event to rally support for the monument. He was hoping to get a check for $50,000 from Sun Oil Company to kick off fundraising," Christian recalled. "He asked if I could attend the ceremony. I get there and there are buses of protestors out front. Most of them were wearing some kind of jungle fatigues. They had a bunch of signs. One said, 'No memorial for pigeon shit.' The Sun Oil speaker backed out when he saw the protestors. Jan asked me to speak in his place. The building was filled up with protestors. I got up to speak and looked out at this room full of ragged warriors, a lot of them Vietnam veterans. I said, 'In this great country, do we need a memorial for pigeon shit?' They all screamed, 'No, no, no.' And then I said, 'In this great country, do we need to remember the sacrifice, the valor, the honor, of our Vietnam War veterans? And they said yes we do. My third thing was, 'In this great country of ours, can we have both things we want – social programs for veterans and a great memorial to honor our dead?' The whole room erupted in cheers. That's how we got started. I had to do something because the guy from Sun Oil might not have given us a check."

Around the same time, in 1979, David Christian made national headlines on Veterans Day. He had been hired by the administration of President Jimmy Carter in 1977, perhaps in a ceremonial gesture to take advantage of Christian's high profile as a Vietnam vet. As Veterans Day approached in November 1979, Christian was asked to give a speech in D.C. on this hallowed day.

"I was told right before the ceremony that the President was showing up and they would have to cancel my speech," Christian recalled in a 1983 interview with PBS. "They asked me to give the Pledge of Allegiance instead. I'm very proud to give the Pledge of Allegiance but I thought, Jeez, I still have my speech in the back of my mind. So when I walked out on that stage, and the President was sitting to my immediate left, I started out by saying, 'It gives me great pleasure to be here today' and I went on to speak for a few minutes about the plight of Vietnam veterans and the social problems they have that are unmet and unanswered. The Secret Service told me later I spoke for three minutes and 49 seconds. And then I led the crowd in the Pledge of Allegiance."

Christian lost his job as an adviser to veterans in the aftermath, although the Carter administration quickly reassigned him to another position in the Labor Department. His actions in front of President Carter all but cemented his place as a hero among fellow war veterans.

Dave's brother Doug was already suffering at this point from a cancer that later would be traced to Agent Orange, which in 1979 had not yet even been acknowledged as a possible killer of American soldiers exposed to the poisonous dioxin in Vietnam.

From 1975 on, as Christian learned more and more about the dioxin that became known as Agent Orange, he testified in front of Congress on numerous occasions, criticizing government reports that tried to downplay the killing effects of the poison that was sprayed from airplanes on to the Vietnam countryside, ostensibly to kill off the vegetation and eliminate hiding places for the enemy on the outskirts of U.S. military bases and camps. The government eventually admitted that during Operation Ranch Hall, from 1961-71, this extremely toxic dioxin was sprayed over 4.5 million acres of Vietnam.

"The government had a report that said the pilots' mortality rate was the same as other people who were not sprayed with Agent Orange," Christian recalled in the PBS interview. "Well, a reasonable person would have to know they weren't spraying Agent Orange around the cockpits of the plane. And that the pilots were wearing protective clothing, whereas the GIs were walking on the ground where the Agent Orange was descending, where it was eating vegetation and turning trees into toothpicks within days."

In 1979, a class action lawsuit was filed on behalf of 2.4 million veterans who were exposed to Agent Orange in Vietnam. Five years later, seven chemical companies agreed to pay $180M in compensation to the veterans or their next of kin. The Supreme Court confirmed the settlement in 1988. But the Veterans Administration still wasn't compensating Vietnam vets for illnesses initially linked to AO – soft tissue sarcoma, leukemia, prostate cancer, Hodgkin's disease and type 2 diabetes. President George H.W. Bush finally signed into law in 1991 the Agent Orange Act, which established links between certain diseases and Vietnam War service. This would begin the process of providing compensation for Vietnam vets impacted by exposure to Agent Orange.

While working for the Department of Labor in the late 1980s, Christian was fortunate to participate in the writing of legislation for Agent Orange and PTSD legislation that would eventually become law and help veterans not only of Vietnam but Korea, WW II and the modern wars in Iraq and Afghanistan.

Over the years, Christian became a polished speaker, and public figure. He ran twice for the Bucks County Congressional seat of

Democrat Peter Kostmayer, winning two Republican primaries. He lost by just 4,000 votes to Kostmayer in the 1984 general election (less than one percentage point).

"Running for office and losing was a most painful experience," Christian admitted. "My campaign did an opposition report that had some negative things to say about my opponent but I chose not to use them in the campaign. I wanted to run on my record, on what I had done in my life. I thought people would vote based on my character. But this was a baptism by fire for me in politics. I think some people had trouble believing my story, that I could become an officer at 18. When mud is thrown in politics, people are sometimes like sheep and they just follow along."

Government work as a consultant would remain a part of Christian's life for the next 20 years. He had taken a course in Russian at Middlebury College and was conversant in both Russian and German.

"The government sent me to Russia before the revolution in 1991," Christian said. "After the revolution, I was the first American sent into Bosnia. That was not an accident. I was sent in there to help set up the infrastructure."

Christian traveled a lot but often had time at home for family and projects. He began writing his autobiography in the 1980s and tried to pitch the finished product to big-time book publishers. In typical David Christian fashion, he marketed the book on his own, walking in the front door of over 200 publishing houses in New York City, without any success, before he hired an agent who hooked him up with McGraw-Hill.

"When I first wrote my book, it was titled, '*Christian's Butchers*,' " the articulate veteran said in 2019. "The book was 500 pages. It was too long for the publishers, too much detail. One publisher told me they had 'stables' of writers who could edit and shorten the book. I got hooked up with a husband-and-wife team up in Vermont. They smoked pot all weekend. I went back to the publisher and said they are not right for me. Then they introduced me to Bill Hoffer (author of *Midnight Express*). They gave him my book. Bill read it and told me we have to cut out the burn section because they can't print that stuff. Hoffer had to cut the book from 500 to 230 pages. The names of my high school friends who came to visit me in the hospital were cut out. A lot of stuff was eliminated from my manuscript."

The book, '*Victor Six*,' was published in 1991 by McGraw Hill. And then it was published in paperback by Pocket Books, a division of Simon & Schuster. It was well received in the community of war veterans. Jan Scruggs, founder of the Vietnam Veterans Memorial, said this about his old friend: "Dave Christian was a significant part of the Vietnam Veterans Memorial effort in Washington. When the memorial came under attack, Victor Six charged forward. The nation and I will always be thankful for Dave's courage."

In 1993, Christian had a chance to experience that surge of adrenalin that comes with combat, only this time the opportunity occurred in the leafy borough of Newtown, Pa.

"My wife had a salon in Newtown," Christian said with a half-smile on his face, recalling this story. "Three guys came in to rob her. I was working on a screenplay upstairs. I came down the stairs and confronted them in the street. One of them said he had a gun."

Christian, sitting in a chair at home, memorabilia from his busy life all around, looks at his interviewer, eyes narrowing, nostrils beginning to flare. He is changing into the young soldier who ran down those two Viet Cong teenagers in the early days of his Vietnam combat tour.

"I told him to take the gun out and shoot me, you mother …. You are not shooting a cherry boy here. Once you shoot me, I am going to take that gun away from you and shove it up your (butt) and blow your brains out. He got kind of scared and began looking for the police. Peggy had called the police while I was outside. I marched these crooks back down the street. When the police arrived, the punks went over to the first car. My guy said to the policeman, 'Please put me in the car. This guy is a frigging nut.' "

The story made for good news in the local newspapers and television station. Nearly 25 years after the war ended, Bucks Countians got a taste of David Christian's essence.

"I am flamboyant," he admitted. "I like being different. I like being a swashbuckler. Sometimes I wear cowboy boots and a big hat. Every one of us has an individual streak in them. Most don't show it.

This is who I am. Elvis once said he never wanted to go somewhere and not be noticed. I guess that's part of me, too."

At the end of the day, Dave Christian wants to be known for his patriotism and love of country, for his love of family and friends. He often visits the Washington Crossing National Cemetery, stopping to stand and reflect over his brother Doug's grave. Christian lives almost within sight of where Washington crossed the Delaware River in 1776. It is not a long stretch of the mind for Dave Christian to think about Washington's soldiers riding in boats on a stormy night, heading over to attack Hessian soldiers in Trenton on Christmas Day.

Christian considers himself a conservative Republican in many ways. But his patriotism and belief in our country's original values always come first.

"I respect the anti-war protestors for standing up for their cause," he said. "That is what America is all about. That's what we learned in the 1960s. Those folks from the 1940s planted the idea in our heads. It is what we believe in our hearts, our minds, our souls. Whatever we believe, we can talk about it. We don't have to always agree. The one great thing that came out of the 1960s is we can agree to disagree. The problem we had was the politicians could not agree on how to fight the Vietnam War. They couldn't make a decision. We needed politicians who would make a stand on the war. As a soldier, I would have been proud of a government leader who acted decisively on Vietnam."

And that's how the war works for most Vietnam veterans, Dave Christian included. We keep fighting it over in our heads. The big difference is that Dave Christian never stops trying to help out his fellow veterans.

"I set up a Veterans Wellness program at the YMCA," he said. "It's for veterans and spouses. People come in for social reasons. They can find out what benefits they might be eligible for. They can exercise, do yoga, get stronger physically and mentally."

The interviewer is done asking questions. It is nearly noon and David Christian is late for work. Still working at 70, he is President of

DAC International Consultant Company, CEO and President of Medical/Surgical Company and owner of DAC-Val hydraulic equipment company, supplying the United States Navy and Air Force.

The kid who hitchhiked to New York City at age 13 has never stopped working. He has been around the world a few times, carving a path that might never been predicted for a youngster who stood in the "poor lines" in Bristol, waiting for surplus food doled out by the government.

The war is never too far from his thoughts. His war. The Vietnam War.

"I weighed 90 pounds when I was first in the burn hospital in Japan," he said. "I was given last rites and was very bitter about it when the priest came around. I did not want his last rites. The priest tried to pacify me by telling me I was lucky because I was already married and had a child on the way. I told him to go away."

David Christian's life can perhaps be defined by the fighting spirit he showed in the face of adversity, from the time he was a little kid, on through the Vietnam War, and then in all the years that followed, as he battled for what he thought was right. He has become a familiar sight all over Bucks County, giving speeches, sticking up for veterans, and never giving up. He is a homegrown treasure, a legitimate war hero, and a man who would always have your back when trouble visits.

PEACE AT LAST – David Christian and wife Peggy pose on the steps of the Philadelphia Museum of Art with four of their grandchildren (Photo courtesy of David Christian)

WORLD CHAMPIONS! — Members of the 1960 Levittown American Little League team gather around Boston Red Sox star Ted Williams in the visitor's dugout of Yankee Stadium after winning the World Series.

CHAPTER TWO
From Little League to Vietnam

Back in the 1950s and 1960s, every neighborhood in Lower Bucks County seemed to have baseball fields and swimming pools filled with youngsters having fun. The towns of Fairless Hills and Levittown were constructed with recreation areas built into the blueprints. This exploratory concept of suburban living depended upon providing positive experiences for a new generation of kids who would become the "Baby Boomers." Most of these youngsters played sports or hung around the swimming pool during the lazy days of summer.

Little League baseball became popular in the early 1950s. A team from Morrisville, right next door to Fairless Hills, won the World Series in 1955 just 200 miles from home, in Williamsport, Pa. Levittown would soon have five Little League programs while Fairless Hills, a much smaller town, settled for one. The fields would vary from pristine to barely above sandlot, depending upon how much time the community invested in growing grass and building fences around these miniature ballparks.

In the summer of 1960, as John F. Kennedy campaigned for President, a Little League team called "Levittown American" repeated the feat of Morrisville, capturing the World Series in Williamsport and bringing extreme pride and happiness to the community it represented.

"I played for Levittown Continental," said Don Bentivoglio, who went from Little League all-star to combat infantry officer in Vietnam between 1960 and 1969. "Looking back, the thing that strikes me is how dedicated the coaches were to us kids. They had day jobs and night jobs but they always managed to get us a lot of practice time and they took the time to coach us on weekday afternoons and weekends. In spite of their personal commitments, they always showed up or arranged for another coach to take over for them.

"During the summer, the kids in my neighborhood of Pinewood tended to meet at the baseball field or the swimming pool, which were right next to each other," Bentivoglio added. "Most sections of Levittown called one of the town's Public Recreational pools as its own. That's where the girls were! But we also spent a lot of time playing baseball and basketball. Our all-star team (based at the Pinewood pool) faced Levittown American in the first round of the tournament when we were 12 years old. We had a good team but American had some stars, guys like Joe Mormello, Jules Kalkstein and Jimmy Grauel. They beat us. I think the score was 7-1. And then they went on to win the World Series. There was no shame in getting beat by the world champs!"

Jimmy Grauel was 12 years old when he played on the 1960 Levittown American squad and just 18 when he jumped off a helicopter into the Vietnam War as an infantryman with the Third Marine Division. Six short years between the innocence of youth and the grim reality of combat.

"As a kid, I did not think winning the World Series was a big deal, at least not until we came home and they had a big parade for us," Grauel said from his home in Las Vegas in February 2019. "I still don't think any of us realized what an accomplishment it was."

Grauel played centerfield and delivered a key two-run double in the championship game at Williamsport, backing up the strong pitching of Joe Mormello, who would also end up in Vietnam as an infantryman with the Army's 101st Airborne Unit.

Another member of the American roster, Rodger Barto, also served in the Vietnam War with the Air Force. Three players out of 15 on the roster. Where 1 in 10 was the national average, it was closer to 1 in 7 for the Pennsbury High Class of 1965 that included Barto, Grauel, Mormello and Bentivoglio. A survey conducted prior to the 50th reunion determined that at least 52 classmates were Vietnam War veterans. There were approximately 350 boys in the class of 725 students. Around 175 served in the military in some capacity, regular service of two or three years, or the reserves, which required only six months active duty but a yearly training camp for six years.

"That's not surprising," Bentivoglio said. "We were a blue-collar town. Not too many of us went off to private colleges. I went to a branch campus of Penn State called Ogontz for two years but my dedication to studies was not great and I dropped out for a semester to figure things out. The draft board figured it out for me and contacted me two weeks after I dropped out of college."

Grauel's future was laid out for him at the age of 16.

"My father told me he couldn't afford to send me to college," Grauel noted. "I had to quit playing baseball and get a job. I had been doing a lot of reading about military history and decided to join the Marines. I signed up in March of 1965 and went into the Marines two weeks after I graduated. Basic training was terrible. But I wasn't shocked by how hard it was. I had researched everything before I went in. I knew they were going to try and break me down. I was in good shape physically. So I got through basic. I was supposed to become a MP (military police) but then the war really got going and they changed my MOS (job) to 03-11, which is infantry."

Grauel fell in love and married his girlfriend, Dorothy, in June 1966.

"I went to Vietnam in July of 1966 and stayed there into August of 1967. Served with the Third Marine Division. Our forward base was at Phu Bai, very near Hue City. My time in Vietnam was pretty hairy. That's how I would describe it. Day and night, we went out on ambushes. We would go into villages where we knew there were VC and NVA hiding out. We worked closely with a Vietnamese militia unit. We actually lived for a while in a village called Ga Xe Lua."

Vietnam took the last vestiges of innocence away from all of these boys who turned into men the moment they reached the war zone.

"I don't regret going into the Marine Corps," Grauel said. "I do have some bad feelings about my Vietnam experience. My worst experience? There was a night ambush where we intercepted a bunch of Viet Cong moving through a village … (long pause) … I take that back. The worst thing for me was after I came home in the summer of 1967. On Sept. 11, our compound was overrun. Five Marines were killed and 13 were wounded. Friends of mine. The way I found out, somebody from my unit came home and got in touch with me, told me that I had lost one of my best friends, Ronald Black. We both liked Motown music. Ronnie was from Chicago."

Grauel's trip back home to the "real world" did not go smoothly.

"We flew into Travis Air Force Base," he remembered. "I was traveling by myself, not with my unit, just a bunch of soldiers returning home from the war. That's how most soldiers came home from Vietnam. The sergeant in charge told us it might be a good idea to change into our civilian clothes before we were bussed to the airport in San Francisco. I did not have any civvies so I rented a cab and had the driver take me to a clothing store."

Soldiers tended to ignore this kind of treatment as they were mainly focused on getting home to the people who loved them. In Jim's case, that would have been his parents, and his wife.

"Dorothy was working at Reedman's (a car dealership) when I called from Chicago," Grauel recalled. "She was out with friends. Nobody knew I was coming home until I made the call from Chicago. My parents had moved to Collingswood, N.J. while I was away. I only went back to Levittown once or twice after I came home. One time, I visited my in-laws. I did not see my old friends back home. Pat Roy, who got killed in Vietnam, grew up in my neighborhood. We used to play basketball over at his house because his parents put up the first hoop on a garage on our street. Pat was a good guy with a great sense of humor."

Grauel's parents picked him up at the Philadelphia airport.

"The first thing they noticed was I had lost a lot of weight. I was down to 155 pounds. I was around 185 when I went to Vietnam."

The war had also taken away Grauel's youthful innocence. He was still only 20 years old, not old enough to vote yet. But he was a hardened veteran of a serious war that half of America, including most people Jim's age, were turning against back home.

"The thing about going to war, what I learned from it," Grauel said, searching for his feelings, "is that the camaraderie I had with my fellow soldiers was the best thing we had going. We were there to save each other's lives. This had nothing to do with politics. Vietnam also helped me to respect other people. The Vietnamese civilians were dying, just like we were. There was no race involved for me."

Little League had been the same way for Grauel and his fellow all-stars. They had each other's backs for 13 games in the summer of 1960.

"I relive those memories every summer when the Little League World Series comes on television," he said. "I played centerfield and hit a two-run double in the championship game. Joey (Mormello) threw a no-hitter and we beat a team from Texas."

The connection between playing team sports and fighting in a combat unit is not as big a stretch as one might think. Don Bentivoglio explained why.

"There's teamwork involved in sports, and in combat," he said. "We learned in Little League that we had to show up for practice, do our best and support our team members. That was part of becoming a team. In those days, the coaches were not afraid to slap you in the back of your head if you acted like an idiot (probably would have been arrested for that today). They taught us discipline at an early age. It was the same in the Army. There were quite a few parallels to Little League. Like any team sport, the Army was all about showing up on time, doing your best because your life might depend on it, and supporting your teammates because their lives often depended on you.

"This showed up in different ways. When we went out on a mission, we collectively made sure everyone had the right equipment because everyone's lives might depend on what the 'other guy' was carrying. We made sure people stayed awake and alert on guard duty, even after humping in the high heat over rough terrain all day. When someone got wounded, the team medic would stabilize them, the med-evac helicopter crews would risk their lives to come in (often under hostile fire) to pick them up and then the doctors and nurses were always standing at the ready when the chopper landed. All of these inter-related components were part of a well-orchestrated and well-trained team. We had so much respect for the courage and dedication they all showed. You always had each other's backs in Vietnam."

Bentivoglio, who would become a First Lieutenant and lead his own platoon in Vietnam, drew a parallel between good sportsmanship in sports and respect for your opponent in combat.

31

"We had a coach in Little League named Jim Toner who always told us to show good sportsmanship, whether we won or lost, and that we always should congratulate the other team. Well, obviously, you could not do that in a war but we all learned to really respect the enemy over there. I know there are a lot of Vietnam vets who still hold negative feelings about the Vietnamese but, in retrospect, I do not see it that way. Their side was fighting for their beliefs (independence and communism) and our country was fighting for our beliefs (which depended on who we were listening to). If there were polls taken during those days, I dare say that the teenage Vietnamese fighters might have wished they were anywhere else, same as ours. If the sacrifices on both sides can ever be rationalized, South Vietnam is now a thriving capitalistic/communist society and our countries are speaking with each other cooperatively. A long way and perhaps a stretch from Little League, but one hell of a life experience that may have begun with our Little League participation."

Don Bentivoglio came home and eventually established himself in the world of finance. (Don has also written his own chapter for this book.) Jimmy Grauel moved out west with his wife and started a family while working in the computer industry.

NEWLYWEDS – Jim Grauel and his wife Dorothy were married before he left for the Vietnam War in 1966. (Photo courtesy of Jim Grauel)

"My wife got a job working for the Department of the Navy and sometimes we would go to parties," Grauel admitted. "I remember someone asking me if I ever killed anyone. I just ignored that stuff. I never talked about the war with anyone, not even my wife. My daughter is going to read a book about my high school and the Vietnam War. I think she will learn a little bit about what I went through from the book. I just don't like to talk about the war."

Jim's wife passed away in 2017. The old soldier now lives with his daughter in the Las Vegas suburbs. His brother Robert also died in 2017, from a cancer in his blood related to Agent Orange exposure in Vietnam.

"Robert was a couple of years younger than me," Jim Grauel said. "He joined the Army and went to Vietnam. He came home and everything seemed fine until this cancer showed up in his blood. They told him it was caused by Agent Orange."

A G.I. NAMED JOE – Joe Mormello won a Little League World Series champion-ship and fought as an infantryman in Vietnam in the early years of his life. (Photo courtesy of the Mormello family.)

Joe Mormello continued his baseball dream after high school, enrolling at Rider College in Trenton, N.J., right across the Delaware River from Levittown. A serious knee injury in his senior year ended Joe's dreams of playing professional baseball. But the injury healed and Joe soon found himself in the Army, trained as an infantry soldier, and heading to Vietnam. Joe was fortunate enough to make it home safely and soon set up a chiropractor business in Levittown that he maintained for 40 years. Joe and his wife Dorothy raised three children and now reside in Point Pleasant, N.J., not far from the ocean, during their retirement years. An illness prevented Joe from contributing to this story but he did provide an Army photo and his wife, Dorothy, gave me background information that proved helpful.

MARINE CORPS TANKER – Terry Wallace, lower right, and a crew mate service their tank during down time in Vietnam. Wallace served in the war zone from Aug. 1966 until September 1967 in the Chu Lai/Da Nang region. (Photo courtesy of Terry Wallace.)

CHAPTER THREE
Terry Wallace Recalls 'The Suck'

BY TERRY WALLACE

Not all of us Vietnam veterans had the same experience, but we all lived in some mix of the heat, noise, sweat, mud, rain, and horror of a tour in that land nearly 10,000 miles from home. I called it "The Suck," which most of us did. Many of us were barely 19, awakened from our adolescence to fight a war we didn't win and then come home (if we did) to a changed America. Many of us had to start over. Some could not. This is how things played out for me.

I was born near Bolivar, Pa, a quiet mining town in the mountains north of Pittsburgh, the first of two children to my Dad and Mom, career military folks who met at a USO dance. My younger sister and I came later.

Bolivar was home to my Grandfather on Mom's side. He was a coal miner as were most of the men in Bolivar. He died of black lung when I was a youngster. Mom had five brothers and four sisters. All but one brother served in the Army, including one in the Korean War's infamous Pork Chop Hill battle. Another, who I never met, died getting off a bus while returning home.

My sister and I spent summers in Bolivar while our parents worked in Philly. Free to roam, I had many adventures hunting and fishing with my uncles. The oldest one, Arthur, was president of the local gun club. He taught me to shoot and load our own ammo. Leonard, the Pork Chop Hill vet, was a little crazy, but my favorite since he took me ground hog hunting. Once he sighted for me as I squeezed off my first and only groundhog kill. Grandma cooked it that very night for dinner!

Bolivar was a place where a kid could roam the hills and valleys wearing a coal miner's hat, carbide lamp and all, carrying a sawed-off shotgun. He could also be adopted by a local stray dog who went everywhere with him and slept on Grandma's porch at night. I was that kid.

Our real home was northeast Philly. We went to school there and made good friends. I threw a fit at eight years old when we first moved to Levittown for better jobs for my parents. A new bicycle cured my fit, and Vermillion Hills became home until my junior year of high school.

Levittown was a great place to grow up. Our back yard bordered a large woods between our street and Fairless Hills which was the scene of exploring, building forts, and even BB gun wars. We played pickup football in a vacant field on the Fairless Hills side. As we got older, driving cars, girls, and the Beatles took over. My best friend and I joined the Falls Township Fire Company when I was sixteen. Firefighting got into my blood.

In junior year at Pennsbury, we moved to an old farm house in Yardley. Old friends still hung out together, and we met new ones. Pennsbury was kind to me even though I wasn't the best student. I was inclined to daydream and get into mischief. The Vice Principal reined me in enough to stay in school. Science and math became more difficult for me each year, and by senior year I had completely alienated the physics teacher. It all worked out with extra studies so that I could graduate, thanks mostly to my Mom.

I was more interested in writing and music. In creative writing class we had listened to Bob Dylan songs for inspiration. I had played the trumpet since fourth grade and was in the band throughout high school, and I also taught myself to play the guitar, which is still a passion for me. I met a girl who could sing like a pro and we fell in love. We would perform at family functions and parties, and were pretty much inseparable. The music lasted longer than the love.

In our family, school and work came first. Both of my parents worked full-time, and I had to support myself through all kinds of part-time jobs, like paper routes, selling newspapers and ice cream, and mowing lawns in Levittown. After high school I went to work full time for a Formica tabletop maker in Yardley.

By then, most teenage boys were thinking about the draft, discussing options like puncturing an eardrum (that would have ended my music career), escaping to Canada, going to college, or joining up. Some gravitated to the anti-war movement lured by the tenor of our era's evolving music and "free" culture. My Mom and Dad lobbied for me to join the Army or Navy, and Mom even made phone calls to a Navy recruiter on my behalf. I said goodbye to my girlfriend and arrived in Philadelphia on Draft Day.

DRAFT DAY

Draft Day (Jan. 3, 1966) resembled a circus lacking only clowns, animals, and popcorn. Crowds of young men were herded into various lines to sign all types of papers and undergo all kinds of examinations. The song *Alice's Restaurant* by Arlo Guthrie describes it well. It was a long process and a long day. There were stations for various types of exams. We were questioned, measured, weighed, poked, and prodded while we shuffled through the lines. Once in a while people would be pulled out and taken to special areas to be examined more closely by special doctors. We would never learn their fate.

One embarrassing exam came when we had to form long lines from one end of the room to the other, pull down our pants and shorts, and bend forward in unison. A doctor, presumably, walked up and down the line peering into our butts. Occasionally someone was pulled out of the line. I'm glad I wasn't one of them.

Finally we were herded into another large room. We were tired and hungry, and it was late afternoon. There were no chairs. After standing around for what seemed forever, a man in crisp green utilities strode in with a clipboard and in a loud voice read off 40 names including mine. We were all drafted into the United States Marine Corps. We were separated from the rest and led into another room where we were sworn in on the spot.

PARRIS ISLAND (NOT A CITY IN FRANCE)

I spent the rest of that evening and night in a plane and on a bus. The bus was very comfortable as it quietly sliced through the southern night. At about 2 a.m. it pulled into Parris Island, South Carolina. The quiet was shattered by a huge foul-mouthed man with a Smokey the Bear hat who jumped onto the bus and barked orders and insults into our faces. We lined up on the famous yellow footprints and were immediately introduced to the hell we had all imagined except worse. We were from New York, New Jersey, Pennsylvania, and surrounding areas, and we knew we were in deep shit.

From that point on, all decisions were made by the drill instructors. All we had to do was execute them perfectly while trying not to stand out. We were shuffled into haircuts, inoculations, dental exams, physical exams, orientation classrooms, and other processing necessities. We no longer recognized each other without hair. We wore our Marine Corps covers (hats) pulled down like duck bills so we would look as ridiculous as we felt. We had determination on our faces and fear in our eyes.

Boot camp was eight weeks long then, instead of the usual 13. That really meant we would learn everything we would need to make us Marines ready for Vietnam in a hurry. To cut no corners there would be no leisure time, not even weekends. Many recruits turned to religion because they could go to church for a half hour once a week if they had time after doing their laundry by hand outside on big wooden benches.

The DI's were always in our faces. To mark their territory they stood us at attention at the foot of our racks (bunk beds), two rows facing each other. The Senior DI walked up and down the line of terrified men, staring each one down and loudly pointing out any peculiarities. We were read the rules, the expectations for Marines, the riot act, and everything in between. Standouts were given cute nicknames, like turd, shit breath, and donut man. The rest were known as pukes or worse. The movie, *Full Metal Jacket*, captures the real thing.

Over the eight weeks we were molded into a well-functioning platoon shaped by rigorous training and constant supervision. We rotated from area to area, always running. We ran from one training venue to another, parade deck to mess hall, and everywhere in between. In fact we ran all the time unless we were practicing drill, which meant precision marching until we got it perfect. Everything we said was prefaced by Sir, and ended by Sir, yes Sir; Sir no Sir; Sir I don't know Sir,

Sir Request permission to speak to the Drill Instructor sir. The fastest of us weren't fast enough; the toughest not tough enough, and the shy, well, they got over it.

We had a few minutes of "free time" some nights before we hit the rack as long as we were polishing our boots, shining our belt buckles or writing letters. One evening during free time I was called to report to the Drill Instructor. I ran down the squad bay at full speed in my skivvies and stood at attention outside the DI's door, tapping as required, and properly requested to speak. I forget the exact reason I was called, but I will never forget the beating I got for not wearing my shower shoes!

We were openly punished for any infractions, missteps, eyeballing, incorrect marching, or not keeping up formations while running. We were harassed individually and as a platoon to immunize us from stress. This weeded out the fragile. It was not uncommon to see a recruit running around the parade deck with underwear on his head, or shouting "I am a Dipshit!" or doing pushups out on the parade deck. Drill cadence called out by the DI's mostly contained slurs about the Viet Cong or warnings about our fate if we did not become "squared away Marines" in a hurry.

An entire creed is built around the Marine and his rifle. The rifle is his life, without it he is nothing. He must know it inside out, disassemble and assemble it, know each part and what it does, and keep it spotless inside and out. He must qualify with it at the range after much practice. All Marines must be at least Marksman level, with two higher levels above it to try to achieve. Rifles were inspected often. They had to be handled and presented properly as learned in rifle drill training. At the time ours was the M14. Ironically, we would transition to the M16 in Vietnam.

There were a few evolutions I will never forget: Forced marches with gear and full packs (don't be the last guy constantly running to catch up!), choking and gagging in the gas chamber, crawling under barbed wire under live machine gun fire, marksmanship qualifying, hand-to-hand combat, and confidence course, which I assume is called the Crucible today. I remember being clobbered in bayonet training, when I was matched with a monster the size of Paul Bunyan. I

41

remember having to dry shave another recruit because he hadn't shaved close enough. Who could forget throwing each other around in hand to hand combat training and being able to break down and reassemble your rifle in the dark? There are many more. You remember boot camp for a lifetime.

We were assigned our MOS and assignment on the last day. Mine was 1811, Tank Crewman, Vietnam. That would guarantee combat but save my life many a time.

ADVANCED INFANTRY SCHOOLS

Next stop, advanced infantry training in Camps Lejeune and Geiger. All Marines are infantryman in addition to any other MOS. At these camps, we underwent weapons training of all types -- live grenades, mortars, machine guns, rocket propelled grenades, and field combat operations training. The M1s which had been used in World War II were issued to us. We had range training there also. M1 was an accurate rifle.

One of my favorite challenges in infantry training was the live-fire exercise where we would walk individually along a narrow elevated Causeway with our M1s while random targets shaped and painted like Vietnamese troops would pop up along the walkway and we had to shoot them. They would jump out from behind a tree, pop up from a hole, or appear behind bushes. After hitting a few targets it was actually fun, like a video game would have been except with a real rifle. The "Gooks" had snarling, evil faces painted on them. Real gooks wouldn't just pop up at you.

Another favorite was a day-long exercise in the woods where we were split into fire teams of four and dropped off miles away in separate locations in the woods. The goal was to find our way back to the starting point without being "captured" by the enemy -- Marine instructors positioned throughout the woods, stalking us. We carried only compasses and our unloaded weapons and gear. We did not know where we were or where the enemy was hiding. We could use only our stealth and hand communication. The stalkers, like those we might find in Vietnam, knew the terrain. Amazingly, as darkness began to fall, my team spotted the home base and we crept to it without any contact with the enemy. In the base all of the captured teams were waiting. It was a proud moment!

A short leave was allowed after Lejeune in order for us to rest, brag to parents and friends, and show off our uniforms.

MACHINE GUN SCHOOL

The California base at 29 Palms was desolate and remote enough for machine gunning. The only palms I saw there were the two holding up the sign. We shot a lot of lizards there. A Tank Crewman would have two machine guns as an extra layer of protection, provided we were IN the tank. But I wouldn't always have such firepower. Also the enemy had figured out how to blow tanks up by then.

29 Palms was a desolate place in the Mojave Desert in California. There was sand, cactus, sun, heat, scrub brush, hills, snakes, lizards, buzzards, and a few animal bones lying around just like in the cowboy movies. It was steamy hot and gritty. Scattered around the base were small Quonset Huts and several other buildings which included a mess hall and sleeping quarters.

We fired 50- and 30-caliber machine guns into the desert. We never ran out of ammo. The 50-caliber is a clumsy and noisy machine that fires large rounds fairly quickly. It usually jammed. The gun also heated up quickly, and required changing out the barrels often. Switching out a hot barrel in the desert is punishing. Actually, all physical effort in a desert is punishing. The 30-caliber was easier to manage. Lizards killed by the 30-caliber died just as quickly. The sand got into the mechanisms and jammed the guns. I have great respect for today's Marines and soldiers who worked and fought in the unforgiving and vast Middle East deserts. Ear protection would have been a nice addition for us, though. What??

TANK SCHOOL, OCEANSIDE, CALIFORNIA

This is where we became one with the tank. We learned everything about the M48 Patton: shooting, driving on all kinds of terrain, basic maintenance, and replacing track sections and road wheels. I learned a 250-pound man CAN fit through the 1-½ foot round escape hatch on the bottom of the tank. The "fat bodies" just had to squeeze more. Speeding along the Camp Del Mar beaches with a 52-ton beast was the most awesome driving experience I have ever had, topped only by tearing through the jungles and breaching rice paddy dikes (which would happen later).

A tank crewman must be capable of serving in all four positions inside a tank: Driver, Loader, Gunner, and Tank Commander (or TC). If any crewman is incapacitated during battle, the stations need to be manned by the other crewmen, as replacements aren't coming. Here are the basic pros and cons of each position as I learned them:

Driver: The most fun and sought-after job in a tank. Driving was awesome. You could see 90 degrees with your head out of the hatch, but much less buttoned up. You could feel the breeze. They had automatic transmissions and steering wheels like cars. One downside was that you had more exposure to landmines out in front, since they usually detonated as you hit them. Another was the weight of responsibility for the lives of the crew while maneuvering in and out of tight spots under fire.

Gunner: The most fun during a fight, since you got to shoot the 90-mm cannon (or the flamethrower on a flame tank) as well as a 30-caliber machine gun. Gunner was the most boring job otherwise, as you sat in a cramped seat down between the hull and the gun and could see or do nothing when not shooting. Sometimes you could sleep on a long drive. Sleep would be in short supply where we were going.

Loader: Great job when on the move. Unlike the Gunner, you had a good view of the countryside when not buttoned up, which was much of the time during travel. Sucky, dirty, sweaty, fast-moving work in a battle, since you had to select the right round, load it into the breach, and load the next, all while dodging the recoil and flying expended shell cartridges, and keeping the 50- and 30-caliber machine guns loaded and feeding properly. Main rounds weighed about 60 pounds each. Don't let anyone tell you that they were a loader on a

44

flame tank because in place of the loader, there was an 80-gallon tank of gasoline and Napalm mix.

Tank Commander: The TC usually was the highest ranked and most experienced of the crew. TCs had charge of all operations, plus radio communications with outside commanders and other TCs as well as internal crew orders. They had to trust the Platoon Leaders and the other TCs and keep the crew functioning as a well-oiled machine. I was never a TC, but I had full respect for them.

All tank jobs could go from routine to full on action in a heartbeat.

CAMP PENDLETON, CALIFORNIA

Staging Battalion at Pendleton was where Marines awaited deployment to Vietnam. Some spent weeks there, some spent months. We were shipped out based on which specialties were most needed. Our days were filled with exercises, forced marches, PT, and formations.

In Staging, we had weekends off. The closest town was Oceanside, a dirty little service town on the beach, crowded on weekends with Marines with crewcuts and a few bucks to spend. There was one movie theatre and many bars and tattoo parlors. There were Marine Shore Patrol police driving around in Jeeps to clean up messes like passed-out drunks, fights, and other misbehavior common in a Marine staging town -- the last American stop for a deploying Marine.

I once almost covered my arms with eagle globe and anchor and bulldog tattoos, but as fate would have it, I drank up all the money first. There were some weekends when we could not afford to leave the base. Absolutely nothing else was going on at Pendleton.

THE SUCK

The Republic of Vietnam (RVN) finally appeared on my horizon in mid-August 1966. After an unremarkable stop at Okinawa, two other tankers and I sat against the bulkheads between cartons of freight on a Cargo plane bound for Chu Lai, Vietnam, worrying about what might lay in store for us. On our approach, the flight crew gave us instructions for arrival, telling us that we were going into a hot zone and that we should keep our heads down and run as fast as we could to the terminal with all of our gear. We clamored out of the plane as ordered into the steamy, breath-choking suck of Vietnam, with the flight crew laughing hysterically above us as we ran, head down, gear flopping, across the tarmac of an almost normal-looking busy airport. Getting the joke, we gathered ourselves, turned, and gave the flight crew the finger as we headed toward the terminal.

We had arrived in Vietnam gung ho and ready to fight. Thirteen months later, if lucky to last that long, we would came home exhausted, wounded or demoralized to a different America. Painful as that was, most veterans would do it again for our country.

SUCK STATION ONE
CHU LAI

A beat-up Jeep picked us up and delivered us to our Headquarters.

We reported to a Gunnery Sergeant (Gunny) as any stateside Marine would do: "Sir, Lance Corporal (so and so) reporting for duty, Sir'!

"Never salute or call anybody Sir," he snarled. "Welcome to 1st Tanks. Get your gear at supply."

We were issued our gear and given a tour of the small compound by a Corporal, who assigned our sleeping quarters in tents.

Chu Lai was in Southern I Corps, the Northern section of RVN that was divided into tactical areas. Our area was busy with work details, tank maintenance, and performing all the necessities needed for living in the field, like showers under aircraft fuel tanks filled with cold water, burning our shit in half-barrels filled with diesel fuel, and urinating into a 4-inch pipe driven into the ground (a piss tube, no maintenance required). At night, we pulled guard duty in the bunkers or in tanks parked around the perimeter. There were four-hour shifts, then relief by another Marine. The perimeter was fairly quiet in Chu Lai, although we heard rounds, mortar fire, and artillery not too far away.

We would light up the night with flares when we heard noises near the wire. There was little sleep in the Suck. We were either bug-bitten or soaked by sweat or the monsoon rains.

Chu Lai was a very short stay for us as our Battalion was moving to Da Nang, further north. It was a lot of work to load up our gear and pack everything for the move. Once everything was loaded and shipped out, the Marines piled into trucks for a drive up the highway to Da Nang. I stayed behind with the party bringing the tanks. It was no easy job to back a tank up a ramp and into an LST ship and secure it. The ramp was moving with the 52-ton weight of the tank and the motion of the ship. We parked them in pairs from stern to bow, fender to fender, securing them with steel cables.

Da Nang was an overnight trip for the Navy LST, which traveled far off the coast before turning north. The weather was rough, with high seas and a lot of wind. You could hear the ship and everything on it creaking with each heave of the waves. Some of us got sick. The sleeping berths were tiny and stacked on top of each other, so most of us shivered on deck in the fresh cold air. In the morning we offloaded in Da Nang and drove the tanks to our new headquarters on a hill near Marble Mountain.

FEARSOME WEAPON – The Flame tank created havoc among enemy soldiers and was the vehicle most frequently targeted for mines on the dirt roads of Vietnam. (Photo courtesy of Terry Wallace)

SUCK STATION TWO
NORTH OF DA NANG

First Tanks occupied a large compound that had been home to another Marine unit. It was a bigger compound with a few rundown hooches which slept about eight Marines each. It took a couple of weeks to get set up, so we worked non-stop. For a while we slept in tents on the ground, four men to a tent. It was monsoon season so we lived and worked in the mud. It was there that a dog found me. Dogs like me. This one was a puppy and he would run off during the day and come back at night to sleep with me. Once he pissed in my bedding. Soon after he stopped coming back I learned that that all the visiting dogs had been rounded up and destroyed for fear of rabies. Dogs were not usually kept as pets by Vietnamese. They were wild, useful, or eaten.

In the compound we maintained the tanks and carried out various assignments. The least popular one was burning the shit, which is just as it sounds. Basically, we set fire to the diesel fuel in the half-drums into which we had expelled our human waste. The barrels were placed beneath plywood platforms with toilet-sized holes cut out. Each day we would drag out the barrels and light them. Billows of smoke rose from the burning shit-fuel mixture, and it needed to be stirred to keep it burning effectively. This had not been covered in the training manuals. It actually WAS shit duty!

Our tanks rolled out each day for missions. We usually accompanied grunts and did a lot of their dirty work while protecting them. Our firepower intimidated the local VC, but we drew a lot of sniper fire and routinely hit the landmines they had planted each night to slow us down or take us out. We took part in Search and Destroy missions as well as larger operations. I started as Loader, then worked my way up to Gunner, then driver. The longer missions lasted anywhere from a couple of days to several weeks. It was a blessing to be on the road and in the shit, as opposed to burning it.

Between field operations we continued to serve on foot patrol duty. At night we either pulled bunker guard duty, went on night patrols or set up ambushes. Our compound was located on a hill about a mile from a well-guarded Seabee fuel dump on another hill. Between the two hills were a jungle, a tiny village, and jungle trails through which the Viet Cong were known to travel. We walked foot patrols in that valley day and night, and set up night ambushes along the trails. It was hot and sweaty work made even more difficult by the bugs and snakes. They hadn't mentioned this in Tank School.

During one patrol just before nightfall, the Seabee Camp guard towers above us opened up on us with automatic fire, assuming we were VC. We dove into the foliage and jungle floor as rounds popped over our head and dug up the dirt near our faces. Our radio man tried desperately to reach our control bunker but could not. Eventually the Seabees stopped firing and we crawled out of there. It is amazing none of us were killed. Friendly fire is an unacceptable way to die, in my opinion. There was hell to pay the next day.

Tank duty took us on day and extended combat missions. We lived on the tanks and ate C Rations which were packed in 1946, the year I was born. They contained 12 varieties of canned food unlike anything Grandma ever made. To this day I will not eat ham with lima beans. C Rations were better when heated, so to heat them we used C4 explosive kept on the tank. Dessert included canned peaches and pears, and each meal came with 4 cigarettes, gum, two tiny sheets of toilet paper, coffee packet, and canned white bread. The bread was inedible, hard as a rock, and tasteless. We threw the hockey puck-sized loaves to hungry dogs along the road and they wouldn't eat them.

Our missions were in various locations, mostly roads but also in mud flats, jungle, and even on beaches. There were always sniper fire and mines to deal with. I once wrote home that they must have had blind snipers, since the shots usually zipped beside or over us or bounced off the tank. Once a group of snipers had the Grunts in front of us pinned down. I was dozing off in the Gunner's hole when The TC jarred me awake over the intercom with "Gunner, rotate left and give me HE at the base of that big tree." I swung the turret and aimed at the base of the tree after confirming the target. The Loader already had the HE (High Explosive) round chambered, and I fired. There was shouting from the grunts deafened by the blast. Not having the tree in my sights anymore, the TC told me it was a direct hit. The grunts told us we took out the tree and left two dead snipers and a blood trail. Such is the life of the Gunner, from boredom to hero in a flash. It's hard to go back to sleep after something like that.

Life back at the compound was work alternating with grunt missions as riflemen. We searched villages and surrounding areas for hidden weapons and VC. Civilians were required to carry government ID, and we had to check everyone we encountered, farmers to children. It felt uncomfortable as a U.S. Marine outsider to demand ID from a Vietnamese citizen living in his home, but orders are orders. Most of us tried to be non-gestapo about it. Those without ID would be brought back for questioning. At night we continued to patrol and set up ambushes. I much preferred the tank operations.

Dogpatch was a small village a short walk from our compound. It had rundown shanties along the main road selling everything you could think of. The people were dirt poor and scratched out an existence by trading with the Americans who had the money. From tea to soda, booze to handkerchiefs, trinkets to porno mags, you could buy it there or they could get it for you. They had dirt floor bars with women, women for "GI, you have good time five dollars," cigarettes, name it. Marines were treated like kings by the villagers as long as we had money. In the market area one would see happy folks, but in reality they weren't. They were dirt poor villagers, robbed and bullied by the VC. In fact, many were VC, smiling in the day and trying to kill us at night.

SUCK STATION THREE
CHARLIE COMPANY, 1ST TANKS

There were four companies in the Battalion, spread out widely over the Da Nang region. C Company's mission was to support the infantry in the field and help defend the air, ammo, and hospital assets at the huge Da Nang Airbase. Located between Marble Mountain and the Airbase, we were a tank scramble away from most threats. In addition, C Company took part in reactionary and planned operations in other areas. Tanks were artillery on tracks, fast and fearsome.

My first assignment there was Driver in the Flame Platoon. Flame tanks were the most feared close-up weapon in our arsenal, able to spew flaming gas and napalm at targets out to 100 yards and in a 365-degree radius. We also had 50- and 30-caliber machine guns. It was hard for the enemy to distinguish Flames from regular tanks because they looked almost identical. But they learned and set their landmines to get us.

We were embedded in all tank operations, going out often in both daily and longer engagements. Sometimes we had to burn bunkers, abandoned or suspect villages, or other enemy assets. When not operating we were cleaning weapons, maintaining and fixing the tanks, target practicing, and playing cards in our hooch. I became just good enough at Idiots Poker to lose money.

My Dad sent a cheap guitar. He had stuffed it with Schlitz beer. It arrived two months later with no strings and no beer. I bought black market strings and entertained and/or annoyed the guys at every opportunity. I carried the guitar strapped to the back of the turret on the longer stay operations. There were a few guys who enjoyed my playing and sang along to the 60's hits of the day. Our theme song was *"We Gotta Get Out of This Place"* by the Animals.

I won't forget an overnight outpost in an area known as the mud flats, where we set up around an abandoned hooch in the middle of a jungle. We were killing time in the hooch when a Tank Commander from another tank said he actually liked the music. He was an easy-going, laid back guy for a sergeant, so we got along. That afternoon he asked if I could teach him to play. I gave him his first lesson, some basic chords. I could tell he could get into the groove.

In the late afternoon we were suddenly called out on a mission. This sergeant commanded the second tank in his platoon. Our platoon was to stand by. We mounted up and were waiting for orders at any minute. Just a few minutes after they pulled out we heard and felt a huge explosion nearby. We thought it had to be an artillery strike. Over the radio a more horrible scenario unfolded. It was worse than we could have imagined.

The second tank had been driving in the tracks of the first, which was standard operating procedure. It was no surprise that the lead tank hit a mine causing minor damage, which happened all the time. My guitar student, the second tank's TC, feared for the disabled tank's driver who had enlisted with him and had been his friend since high school. He had jumped off his tank to check on him and landed directly on an anti-tank mine and was blown to smithereens. I learned from the Corpsmen that only bits of his torso remained. I have remembered this incident for all these years. I had lost my first and only guitar student to a landmine undoubtedly planted to take out the second tank, which was usually the dreaded Flame Tank.

I had a motto in Vietnam which I often preached to others. Don't make friends. I know that sounds harsh, but with the randomness of deaths and injuries to our personnel it made sense. So many of us lost close friends to death or injury, never to be seen again. My solution, impractical and callous as it sounds, was what I actually believed and preached at that time. Of course we made some friends anyway, but it was tough to lose them. Later in life I would have a lot of trouble with friendships.

One night we were hit by snipers from just outside the wire. We returned fire and the attack subsided. The next day, while patrolling outside the compound, we located three of the snipers' dead bodies and brought them back to our area for identification before turning them over to the locals. On patrol a day later we drove past a festival of some kind being held on a beach. We went closer to investigate, and learned that it was a funeral for the VC we had killed. There were many forms of karma in Vietnam.

Near that same beach we came under heavy fire from a small village. Our tanks were patrolling some 200 yards from the village, and our grunts were pinned down. Requesting permission to fire was necessary because it was an occupied village. Before we could get the green light, however, the entire village suddenly erupted into huge flames from one end to the other in a violent line of explosions. The roar of the departing Phantom jet punctuated a scene of unimaginably horrible death for combatants and villagers alike in the napalm strike we had just witnessed. We could feel the wave of intense heat from 200 yards out.

At some point in most tours, R and R trips were offered to Marines on a rotation basis. These trips were greatly anticipated and wildly hyped. It was expected that in any of the Asian countries to pick from such as Bangkok, there were females eager to shack up and cook for you for a week for very cheap. "You have beaucoup romance with me, GI." R and R flights were free. A Marine could save up his pay and come back broke but in love with one of these lovely ladies, who would already be getting ready for the next GI. I knew a guy who went to Bangkok for R&R. He came back a new man, madly in love with his Asian girl and vowing to go back to marry her. He may have tried this, since he went AWOL and never came back.

I chose an in-country R and R for a more restful venue like binge drinking at Red Beach. There, Marines and GIs played football on the beach and took in the scenery. Unfortunately, I came back with a busted lip from tackle football and an injured knee from jumping off a truck into a fight. In hindsight, maybe I should have shacked up instead. My girlfriend back home had stopped writing by this time anyway.

Getting short (that is a month or less to go on your tour), I ran over a landmine driving my Flame tank. It was not a routine mine that took off some track. It had been a large artillery shell or bomb that had been set or command detonated to take out the flame tank, usually the second in the column. We were running almost full speed down a hard dirt road when, suddenly, everything went black for me. I heard no sound, saw nothing, and had an eerie sensation that my tank was flying through air. I don't know how long this lasted, but when I came to I heard excited voices and smelled the unmistakable odor of explosives. The first thing I saw and heard were guys clamoring down to my compartment to check on me.

After being helped out, the only thing I remember was being extremely pissed that my tank had been hit. I took it personally. I was determined to see what had happened and walked around the tank surveying the damage and swearing that I had been tracking the front tank as I was supposed to be doing, so why us? The crews were off to the side of the tank shouting at me to get off the road. I guess in my rage I had forgotten what had happened to my dead guitar student.

When they coaxed me back they were looking at me cautiously. I figure I was a sight, shouting and gesturing and wild-eyed. I don't know when I regained my composure, nor how that tank and I got back to our compound. I remember very little about the rest of my tour, actually. I was amazed to learn the extent of our damage, and still have many pictures. The blast had hit underneath my driver's compartment. It had ripped off the left track, the first three road wheels and support rollers, fenders, and warped the steel hull under my seat, ejecting the escape hatch. That might explain the sensation of being airborne.

The tank had been destroyed. My bell had been rung hard enough to forget most of my last days in the Suck. I do recall the night we were thrown out of our cots by the rocketing of the airbase from just outside our perimeter. We mounted up in moments to return direct fire, but never got permission from command. We were pissed. Denial or delay of permission to engage from remote command bunkers was frustrating, and, in some cases, deadly. I learned that this is inherent in any command structure since eyes on the ground can't see the entire picture in that instant.

I think I lost my head for a while. The only memory I have of my final month is the pilot of the commercial airliner announcing the California coastline in view to our right. I would only find out later in life how much I had actually lost. I still had time to serve and was assigned to Camp Lejeune. There was nothing to do for us returning combat soldiers. We milled around like walking wounded, doing odd jobs on base and drinking in the nearby town at night. The Corps tried as best as it could to get me to re-up, finally even offering me a place in the Marine Corps Band due to my music background, to which I said, "Not a chance!" They gave me an early out on Dec. 23, 1967 for Christmas.

I am by far not the only one who lost part of himself in Vietnam. More than 58,000 brothers lost all of themselves. I am also not the only one to have had a rough transition back to the world. Just ask anyone at the VA how many of us still carry mental and physical scars, need treatment, or are dying off due to service-related diseases, addictions, and suicide.

I am one of the fortunate ones. Most of us tried for years to keep Vietnam out of our heads. For many, there could never have been enough money, whores, promotions, or anything else to make us miss our flight dates. There were some who felt differently, who were gung-ho and drawn to the sights, sounds, and smells of battle, and we needed them. They were the true heroes. Many of their names are on the Wall in D.C. Some of the rest of us carry survivor's guilt and some scars. As Forest Gump would say, "That's about all I have to say about that."

BACK TO THE WORLD

We were all changed, some more than others. Friends were gone or serving, Jody had apparently nabbed our girlfriends (even my singing partner, I guess), and nobody talked much about the war. In many ways we no longer fit in. Young adults had turned to drugs and the freewheeling peace movement of the Sixties, and wanted nothing to do with veterans. Returning vets were harassed, so we avoided wearing our uniforms. We had lost touch with most of our generation. Even the returning vets were set apart by their MOS or extent of combat. If you had been anything but a grunt in the field, you were mocked and looked down upon in many conversations with veterans.

I went astray for a couple of years, as did many of us. Drinking and directionless, I stumbled in social situations and avoided discussing my service. I held many jobs to support myself, but usually lost them or quit after a short time. I suffered from flashbacks and the startle reflex that comes with loud noises. Thunder and fireworks were hard to endure.

Eventually, with the urging of a potential father-in-law and some help from the GI bill, I attended Bucks County Community College and went on to a four-year school from there. I never really stuck to a specific major, trying several and becoming disillusioned in many. For example, in Education class the professor took me aside and told me that I would "never be one of them." I liked journalism until I found out that writing is the easy part but getting the story published was difficult. Like today, editors left a large imprint on your work. In the early

1970s, the VA was keen to pay for graduate programs in rehabilitation. I followed that path into a long career in medical management.

Vietnam kept its hold on me for a long time and still does. I have ever since focused on completing the mission, not necessarily the relationship building and social skills that lead to advancement. My management career was successful despite that. Learning to adapt to change was key, and I had been taught well in the Marines. Having no fear was a blessing.

Here I am in my 70s, retired with a wife and family. I look at Vietnam as a defining moment in my life. I no longer brood about it. Things like noises, crowds, occasional bad dreams, and rain still affect me, but otherwise the years have been good. I wonder where life would have led me if I had not been in the Marines or Vietnam. I think perhaps I am in many ways a better place because of it.

LOOKING GOOD – Terry Wallace shown in his Army days and more recently. (Photos courtesy of Terry Wallace)

(EDITOR'S NOTE: Terry Wallace, Class of 1964 graduate of Penns-bury High, has been transcribing his thoughts about Vietnam in recent years and agreed to share them in this book.)

A GOOD SOLDIER – Brian Delate came home from Vietnam and became an actor, playwright and screen writer. Brian wrote his own tribute to combat veterans called "Memorial Day," a one-man show that he performed in Hanoi in 2013.

CHAPTER FOUR
"You're Just Not ..."

BY BRIAN DELATE

"The two most powerful warriors are patience and time"
~Leo Tolstoy

It's June of 1967 and I park my yellow 1960 Austin Healy Sprite in the shopping center in Trenton, New Jersey. It's my first date with Carole, who is a knockout; blond, buxom, and so nice. We're going to see the World War II movie *The Dirty Dozen*, which just opened. We get the last two seats, and fortunately they're together. The movie is a real crowd pleaser. Later that warm night, as we sit on her porch, I tell her how I'm starting college the next day. I want to sound important and smart, which deep down I feel I'm not. We kiss goodnight and there is magic.

The next morning I drive to Rider College in Lawrenceville, New Jersey. I really want to succeed, but I feel the shadow of failure. I barely graduated from high school the week before, and my fear is that once again the truth about how stupid I am will be revealed. The deal is, I am enrolled for four weeks, five days a week, to take three classes, and I must manage at least a 'C' in each class. If I do, I'll be admitted as a fulltime student in the fall and will then have the valued 2-S student deferment, which would keep me from being drafted into the army.

The war in Vietnam is raging at this time and the anti-war movement is beginning to gain more and more momentum. I know a few guys who graduated the year before from the class of '66, who either were in Vietnam or were going. My dad is a World War II veteran and doesn't seem to have that much of an opinion about the current war, but I recall him reflecting on occasion, '...This war might not be ours.' That was a surprise.

My father played tennis with one of the trustees at Rider and that's how the whole thing came about. I attend my three classes each morning, and then shoot back over the Delaware River to Morrisville, Pennsylvania, where I am a lifeguard at a large apartment complex swimming pool. At night, I see Carole, drink beer with my friends, or attempt to do homework.

From the first day with my classes, I am once again numb to the learning experience. Honestly, I am baffled. Part of the problem is that I am a pathetically slow reader. Unlike high school, where I didn't really care, now I am really trying to succeed and learn. My classes are English Composition 101, History of Western Civilization, and Introduction to Psychology. Despite the fact that I'm not able to grasp the academic tasks, I enjoy the role of a college student. I walk around the campus with pride and purpose, with books and notebooks under my arm. At times I even appear to be deep in thought.

About halfway through the four-week experiment in educational futility, my parents ask me how it's going. I tell them it's a challenge, but that I am making it happen. I guess I was kidding myself, because I could see the writing on the wall even then. I finished with two 'Fs' and a 'D.'

'See I told ya, man!' barks in my mind.

At the end of the four weeks I sit down with the Dean for a brief conversation. "You're just not college material, Son."

He said it so matter-of-factly and then added, "If you're interested in a trade school there are some good ones in the area."

I left his office feeling like the evidence was crystal clear. 'Not college material.' Okay. It was difficult to accept that the proof was clear, and that I was certifiably and genuinely stupid. And I was really trying this time! Damn.

The rest of the summer I lifeguarded, and as Carole became my girlfriend, we started to bond beautifully from the neck down. That autumn, my uncle helped me to get a job at E.J. Korvette, a big, discount department store, working in the record department. I worked full-time, saw Carole, and hung out with my friends. Because the record department had a great sound system, I listened enthusiastically and with great joy to everything from The Doors and The Beatles, to Sinatra and Sergio Mendez.

As far as the war in Vietnam went, I thought, 'That thing will calm down before too long and I won't get drafted.' There were a lot of guys who had made their way to a college or ran to the National Guard and, of course, some went ahead and enlisted. In the spring of 1968, I was called down to Philadelphia to get a physical and do a written test. When I passed, my 1-A draft status was firmly established. I knew that I'd be called in a matter of months. Everybody's guess was that it would be in the coming fall.

As the summer progressed I decided not to wait, and signed up for induction at the end of August. I quit my record store gig, took odd jobs, and enjoyed my time with Carole. We laughed and made love often, and on the morning of August 30th, 1968, she drove me to the train station. We held hands and kissed goodbye. Neither of us had the words, but I think we both knew that things would never be the same.

***

From the first weeks of basic training, I was surprised to see that I excelled in almost every area; leadership, drilling and physical prowess. I was an expert shot with any weapon I touched, and in the immortal words of my tyrannical drill sergeant, "That son-of-a bitch can low crawl faster than a fuckin' rat!" I never imagined I would thrive within such a structure. In fact, I was encouraged to go Officer's Candidate School. 'Who, me?' I seriously considered it, and my father encouraged me. Upon reflection, I can see that he was proud. It occurred to me that maybe I wasn't so dumb, but, oh God, did I miss Carole!

The war, it turns out, and living in an arena that continues to challenge the limits of human experience, becomes the most defining event in my entire life.

***

A year later, at the age of twenty, I return home from Vietnam as a decorated non-commissioned officer. One of the heartbreaks I contend with is losing the connection I had known with Carole. She waited for a whole year, and along with my mother, wrote to me almost daily. Upon my return Carole and I saw each other, but with having been apart for so long, and with the changes I had gone through, our relationship becomes a volatile series of breaking up and making up.

That year back home was a different kind of nightmare. I had to spend the remaining months of my time in the army in New Jersey, and I was able to live off base near home, but found myself drinking heavily. Somehow I was able to do my work at Fort Monmouth, but soon became unreliable as a boyfriend, a son, and a friend. A dark pit inside me was growing. I was angry and depressed, and felt like an outsider with no purpose whatsoever. My rage at myself, and the world, made me feel like killing or getting killed. In Vietnam, all I wanted to do was live, and after coming home, all I wanted to do was die. I grew to hate the army and I wanted out.

When I saw guys going into college from the service, I considered it. Of course I remembered what the Dean had said, 'You're just not college material.'

I had always been a terrible reader. I was super slow and my comprehension pathetic. But what if it could be fixed? I learned that I could leave the army a few months early if I went to college, though deep down I still felt inadequate and insecure about furthering my education. After all, I had already failed in college before.

At the time, I took note of what was going on in my life. I was self-destructing and attracting a lot of X-rated people. Carole stayed away from me more and more. One night I was drinking a load of tequila with a couple of guys, when we decided go over to Trenton and get some wings to eat. At three a.m. standing at a run-down counter on Perry Street where whites seldom dared to go, a black couple came in arguing and pushing each other. A couple of guys pulled the man away from her and he left, but not five minutes later, he returned with a pistol and shot her twice in the chest right in front of us. The soldier came alive in me and I sobered up instantly, dragging my two drunken friends out of there, saving us all.

That night and the next day I seriously wondered what the hell I was doing. 'I can't live like this.' In the short time since I got home, I'd already wrecked four cars, got into a couple of violent scrapes, and made a few appearances in front of the local judges. Plus, I was getting tired of all the fantasies I had about taking myself out. That moment sealed the deal. The local community college was offering an experimental three-part reading program, and I thought, 'If I want to give myself a real chance to succeed, I have to try this.'

Thank God the Army released me, and on June 1st, 1971 I enrolled in the reading class as well as a basic grammar class at Bucks County Community College in Newtown, Pennsylvania. Both classes were zero credits, but I didn't care. I now had a chance to see what it would be like to live on a level playing field with academia. I took a reading test that first day, and Doctor Rosella, who had also been in the military, asked me to stay after class for few minutes.

With real kindness he asks, "Brian, do you know what your reading level is?"

"No, but I know it's not good."

"It's fourth grade."

"Whoa... I knew it was bad, but that is... that's bad."

"Yes it is, but the good news is that we're going to turn this around. Just do what this program asks you to do and watch what happens."

The reading class with Doctor Rosella became a revelation and changed my life. I went from a fourth grade reading level to having an incredible range of college level reading skills. Apparently, ever since I was a kid my eyes would surround each word as I read, which accounted for the slowness. Then my mind would become bored and wander. This was just one example. I learned a variety of ways to read textbooks, and also learned how to speed-read. I felt like Helen Keller when she finally understood that she could speak with her hands and fingers.

I started my first semester in earnest that fall at Bucks County Community College, where I was actually learning; learning how to write and learning what great minds thought. I was even absorbing mathematics. Algebra and trigonometry became fun! 'What!?' Thank you, Doctor Myron Kaplan. Between having my reading re-aligned and a good work ethic from the army, I thrived as a student. 'Who is this guy?'

I got involved in student activities, especially the Cultural Affairs Group. Spent time with Issac Asimov, Robert Bly and many others who visited the college. I felt like I had found a purpose beyond the army and the war. I loved it! I also made a decision to stop listening to pop and rock music. No more Janis, no more Who, no more Doors, no more Creedence. Well, I might have made an exception with Creedence. I vowed to only listen to the music of Mahler, Brahms, Wagner, Mozart and other classical composers. The music, to me, was pure passion, and it reached me deeply.

My friends felt I was eccentric and even a little odd. I didn't care. I found a purpose in college as I had never known. Carole and I had been hanging on by a thread, but then my changes became too much for her. Following your bliss certainly ain't easy.

In my second year at Bucks I decide to take an acting class. I thought this would be fun and light, ha ha, but I quickly learned that I'd be taking risks that would scare me like nothing since the war. The difference was it was a fear that I felt I could learn from, and I did. After my freshman year I was seriously contemplating pre-med, something I'd fantasized about as a kid, however this class with my first acting teacher, David Dean, changed my life yet again.

Halfway through the next semester of that second year at Bucks, I applied to a couple of four-year colleges to complete my education. At the same time I heard there was a very active theatre department at Rider College, where five years earlier I was told that I wasn't college material. 'Hmm...' They had a great program, with a couple of professionals on the faculty. I visited there a handful of times and liked it even more. And it was close to home, so I wouldn't have to move. I applied.

A few weeks later I thought, 'Oh no, you won't get accepted, because they know who you really are, Dude.' After obsessing like this for a couple of days I called admissions at Rider to see what's happening. Over the phone a soft-spoken woman says enthusiastically, "Oh,

Hi Brian, you've been accepted! We just haven't gotten your letter in the mail yet."

Oh, my God! I'm going back to Rider!

***

It's ten o'clock on a cold morning in January in 1975. I sit at a conference table in the administration building at Rider College. At the table are two Deans, two Professors, and two other students. I'm about to go into my last semester before graduation. I'm being nominated to the *Who's Who of Colleges and Universities for 1975,* and have landed a plumb directing internship with McCarter Theatre at Princeton University. Lucky me!

Dean Iorio, stocky build with a husky voice is a thoughtful communicator. He starts the meeting. He says, "Dean Van Der Hyde and myself selected those of you present here today to form a consensus with the sixty-two names on this list."

Everyone is handed a list.

He continues, "We need to decide of these students on the list, who stays and who goes. They are all on probation."

Janet, a tall, slender and well-dressed science major offers, "Are we deciding based on their GPA's?

Dean Iorio replies, "That's a good place to start."

My mind spins, 'Whoa, wait a minute...' And I hear the echo of what was said to me in that summer of '67. Dean Iorio sits across from me. I lean back, raise my hand and pipe up.

"Doctor Iorio, I need to say this. I was here at Rider seven years ago for a summer program of three courses to determine if I could be a fulltime student. It didn't work out for me, and I was told that I just wasn't college material. But, I'm sitting here today, and I wonder, has anybody talked to these people?"

Doctor Iorio nods his head slowly, and then firmly brings his hand down on the table. "That's it, we stop right now." He indicates to the lists, "I'll take those back."

He looks around the table briefly, "This is what we're going to do. I want the resident supervisors to sit down with each person on this list." He nods to me, "Thank you, Brian."

As we put on our coats and gather our things to leave, I decide to hang back. Doctor Iorio does as well. He notices the two albums of Mahler symphonies I have with my notebook. He says, "So, you like classical music?"

"Yes, I do."

As he pulls out his pipe and prepares it for a smoke he adds, "Do you know the Shostakovich Fifth Symphony?"

"Not yet."

"You're a veteran, aren't you?"

"I am."

"That symphony is somber and about suffering, but full of beauty and passion. And I can't tell you how important it was for you to be here today."

As he starts to leave I say, "College didn't only add to my life, Doctor Iorio, it changed it."

"I can tell."

We shake hands and I leave. As I head for my car to make the five-mile drive to Princeton, I realize how fortunate I am, and hope that some of those students who were deemed not to be college material, will get another chance as I have.

EDITOR'S NOTE: Brian Delate continues as an actor to this day. He has appeared in film, theatre and television. His movie credits include Shawshank Redemption and The Truman Show. Brian has also developed his skills as a writer and director. His film, "Soldier's Heart," dealt with the subject of Post Traumatic Stress Disorder. His play, "Memorial Day," focuses on the story of a Vietnam Vet on the verge of suicide as Memorial Day nears. He has performed this play around the country and took it to Vietnam in 2013.

MAKING MUSIC – Liza Hamill graduated from Syracuse University in 1969, earning her diploma during a hectic time in America when college students protested the Vietnam War while some of their friends fought in it. (Photo courtesy of Liza Hamill)

CHAPTER FIVE
The War Affected Everyone

BY LIZA HAMILL

A bit about me ...

I spent my wonder years in New Jersey in one of those post-WWII developments of identical suburban houses. It was within five or ten minutes from all my grandparents, aunts and cousins and overrun with the first ranks of the Baby Boomers. Since I was an only child, I was bereft when my father got transferred to seemingly far away Pennsylvania just before the beginning of ninth grade. It was a rural community there and I knew no one. I was never very outgoing and it was the first real challenge I ever had to face, finding my way when everyone was a stranger.

Even before the mover's boxes were all unpacked my mother died suddenly of a brain aneurism. I went to bed one night and during the night she became ill, was moved to a hospital and I never saw her again. It was that quick.

Within days the divorced woman next door arrived with a casserole. My father was understandably inept at being a home maker so anyone supplying food was a godsend. It didn't take long before I saw where things were headed. One night my dad announced they were getting married. She was so unlike my mother in every way I couldn't imagine what life would be like with her and I told him how I felt. He wasn't an ogre but also wasn't the world's greatest father. He told me he didn't care what I thought and we never discussed it again.

They were married within the year and I found myself in yet another new house and living with two stepbrothers. I probably was not the most pleasant teenager to have around. Are any teenagers pleasant? My mother and I had been extremely close. She had been my best friend and I felt somehow disloyal when my stepmother entered my life.

I was pretty oblivious to the goings on in Southeast Asia when I was in high school. Most of my friends were bound for college so war didn't seem much of a threat to them as it was for some others. At home we seldom discussed college. My stepmother was actively working to get her son into school but my father must have thought I had the smarts to figure it out for myself. I didn't have the sense to seek out a guidance counselor.

The only direction I got was from my boyfriend's mother who suggested Syracuse University because they had a good art school. I applied, got in, and by some miracle qualified for a scholarship that covered about half the cost of my tuition. My father was willing to cover the difference. Suddenly the looming threat of having to look for a job and make a life was postponed four years.

When I left for college my father took me aside and told me that whatever happened, if I flunked out, if I got arrested, if I got pregnant, to not bother calling home because it would be my problem, not his. With those fatherly words of advice I went off to college, clueless about the world, thrilled to be away from home and terrified of screwing up.

PETE...

My freshman year at Syracuse would have seemed perfectly normal if I hadn't been in the art school. While the other girls in my dorm were joining sororities and going to fraternity mixers, typical behavior for "the Greeks," the people I spent my time with were artists, musicians and otherwise colorful types commonly known around campus as "the freaks."

The dining hall was the center of my social life. We'd have dinner and then sit around drinking coffee until they threw us out. It was an opportunity to meet guys. There were no co-ed dorms back then but we all had to eat together and it was there that I was introduced to Pete. One of my classmates said he had asked who I was and offered to engineer an introduction.

Pete started joining us after meals and after some initial flirting he finally asked me out. He was two years ahead of me, an "older man" and very cute. He had the greatest, biggest smile. He had a car, a rarity on campus at the time. He was sweet and funny and best of all was front man for an eight-piece soul band. He too was an art student and won national awards for his illustrations. He seemed to be the whole package.

We dated through the end of my freshman year and saw each other during the summer. By the next fall we were definitely an item. It was only then that it hit home that Pete was going to graduate at the end of year and once he did he'd lose his college deferment. My relative obliviousness to the war in Vietnam was suddenly replaced by sheer panic that they were going to draft Pete.

One of the things Pete and I didn't see eye to eye on was religion. I had been raised a Protestant in a very vague, live and let live sort of way and Pete was raised a devout Christian Scientist. We barely talked about it but I knew he disapproved of any medicine I took and wasn't too happy when I had a drink. When I realized the jeopardy he would be in at the end of the school year I asked him what he planned to do about the draft. He said his religion required him to be a conscientious objector but he wouldn't do anything to avoid the draft. By this time we had friends who were heading for Canada, cutting off toes or just disappearing to parts unknown where Uncle Sam couldn't find them. One character, trying to be designated unfit to serve, legally changed his name to "Grim Reaper." I wanted to know what Pete's plans were. Sadly he didn't have any.

He felt that God would handle things and Pete would follow God's path. We argued about it, me against God. I was disappointed in him for not being more proactive. I didn't understand how he could just wait for the draft board to gobble him up when he could morally and honestly apply for conscientious objector status. The fact that this great guy with so much talent was going to graduate and not even bother to try to save himself made me disappointed and scared. I had just lost the person closest to me a few years before. I didn't want to lose Pete.

He had several months before Uncle Sam finally got him and he spent that time between his home and the campus just hanging around. When he was finally told to report he asked me if I would wait for him and I didn't know what to say. He'd never even said he loved me or talked about marriage. I'd have waited if he had, but as it was I didn't know what I'd be waiting for. I said I didn't think I could. He left and I cried for three days.

After that I didn't hear anything from him until I bumped into him three years later. I was married then and we were both attending an auto race at Watkins Glen. A lot of the Syracuse crowd was there and suddenly there was Pete. It was awkward. He said the Army had made him a quartermaster and he hadn't been required to carry a gun but had been close to the fighting.

If you're trying to have a deeply personal conversation, a race at Watkins Glen with your husband glowering in the background isn't the best venue and we left a lot unsaid. I was so happy to see him home and safe and was willing to admit that maybe God did have a hand in it. Yet with all his talent he was content working as a night security guard at the Christian Science Center in Boston. It seemed like an awful waste to me.

Many years later after the world became digitized I tried to look him up and see how life had treated him. The Syracuse alumni directory just had him listed as "deceased." So many years later and he still made me cry.

ANDY...

My sophomore year I was hit with a bad case of mononucleosis. I was laid up in the infirmary for a week and missed too many classes to catch up so I had to attend summer school. I hadn't been there more than a day or two, too soon to have met the other girls on my floor, when I heard a shriek and the sound of someone sobbing her heart out. I went out into the hall and found that one of the girls had just been told that her fiancée and high school sweetheart had been killed in Vietnam. That was the moment when it all became real for me.

She became one of my best friends and we spent a lot of that summer together. The social fabric was coming unraveled all over the campus and not least among the "freaks." One woman, much more po-litical than I, was collecting weapons under her bed for the coming "revolution." Between the war, civil rights and women's equality there was hardly a day when you couldn't go and protest something.

My friend was mourning her fiancée. She was understandably against the war. There were many urban legends of things a person could drink or eat or do that would cause them to flunk the physical and we spent many sleepless nights pouring weird herbal teas into some poor guy whose physical was the next day. They never worked. "Rec-reational" drugs were pervasive. Everyone was getting nervous.

That included Andy, who lived with his family on a farm out-side of the city. He, too, was an art student, a year ahead of me, and a few of the artist types had taken up residence for the summer in a di-lapidated barn on Andy's family farm. As I recall, there was a sink and a few bare lightbulbs but little else in the way of amenities. One wall of the barn had rotted away and the view from the hayloft out over the fields was gorgeous if you could ignore the gnats and pigeons. Andy's dad made barrels of hard cider and every now and then he'd roll one into the barn, tap it, and walk away. His uncle made something called "scotch" that was 180 proof and occasionally, having tasted a bit too much of it himself, he would put on his kilt, march out into the field and play his bagpipes by moonlight. It was a world away from the trou-bles on the campus

I'd heard tales of this wondrous barn but lacking transportation hadn't visited it until one day I and some friends decided to hitchhike out to see it for ourselves. We had no idea where we were going but we eventually found it, too late to get back to campus that night. We drank some cider, shared a watermelon for dinner and eventually I grabbed an old blanket and crawled off into the hay to sleep. I woke up the next morning to Sergeant Pepper blasting "Good Morning" at ear-splitting volume on the stereo and creating panic among the pigeons.

Andy gave us all a ride back to campus and we had a chance to talk. He was trying to decide what to do with his graduation looming. He had researched his options, getting advice from whoever was offer-ing it and as the months went on he grew a long mop of curly black hair and a bushy beard a pelican could have made a nest in. Everyone had long hair by then. It may have been to annoy our parents, or make us look different from "the establishment," or to poke a finger in the eye of the draft board. Whatever the reason, Andy was growing one of the biggest fluffiest heads of hair on the campus.

By second semester, Andy had made up his mind to go to Canada but had to wait until classes were over so he could get his degree and he was starting to sweat. We all respected his decision. We all felt it was a morally acceptable thing to do, just another form of protest. I don't remember ever hearing any of my crowd disrespecting the boys who fought in Vietnam. I do remember fierce anger at the government in creating a situation where young men had to choose between going to war or avoiding it.

One day in May there was a knock at my door. When I opened it, there stood a young, neatly dressed, clean-shaven fellow with a fresh haircut and oddly familiar glasses who, until he spoke, I didn't recognize as Andy. I cried, we exchanged addresses and hugs and he left for Canada the next day.

Andy   wrote and told me how lonely it was up there. He missed his family and friends. He was staying in a combination hostel/rooming house with a bunch of other American boys in the same situation. Some people called them traitors and cowards for making the choice to go to Canada but in Andy's case I always felt that he gave up a large part of his life to follow his conscience. I will always believe this was the case for a lot of the "draft dodgers." They felt the war to be immoral and they just refused to fight. Some went to prison, some went to Canada.

That summer I'd been the victim of a mugging in Hyannis, Massachusetts while walking home from work one night. I spent several days in the hospital recovering from knife wounds. The hospital had to call my father and, typically thinking like a man of the '60s, he assumed I'd been asking for it although the man I described to the police was eventually arrested on suspicion of killing two other women on Cape Cod in the same time frame. He killed himself in prison. As soon as I was out of the hospital I went back to my job and back to having to walk home in the dark every night. I felt scared and sad and needed a friend as badly as Andy did.

At the end of the summer I hitchhiked to Boston and got on a Greyhound Bus that eventually dropped me off in St. John, New Brunswick where Andy picked me up. His room was small and shared with four guys. Most just had the clothes on their backs since a suitcase would have given away their reason for crossing the border. Once there I could see that his problems were worse than mine so I downplayed my summer adventure. All the guys were very unhappy living in limbo in Canada and I was relieved when my long weekend was over and I could return to Syracuse.

Life was getting weird for all of us. Paranoia was rampant. Phones were assumed to be tapped. There was fear that the government was spying on us and Andy's letters stopped. I never heard from him again.

NELSON...

As my senior year came to a close things were really getting tense. Every semester break college students and thousands of others would meet in New York for huge anti-war demonstrations. My friend, the one whose fiancée had been killed, was by then living in New York City and always kept lumps of sugar in her pockets for the police horses. At one demonstration a cop thought we were giving his horse LSD and we nearly got arrested. Some of my friends were getting pregnant so their boyfriends wouldn't get drafted. More and more friends were headed for the border. In my circle people were pairing off and making plans and getting married. My four-year extension on having to grow up was about to expire too. I met Nelson toward the end of that year.

Desperate times call for desperate measures. He was a big guy and a good artist. We were both single so we became a couple. The fact that my friends seemed to like him led me to believe he was a good guy and wouldn't treat me badly. I can't say I was madly in love but I didn't want anything bad to happen to him either. We decided to get jobs in Syracuse and rent a room for the summer after graduation and we talked vaguely of getting married while he waited to hear about an award that was given every year by the University Art Department. It was a Fellowship to study art in Europe for a year which would get him out of the country and away from Uncle Sam.

When it was announced that he'd won the award I knew I wouldn't see him for a while but at least I knew he'd be safe. When the day came for him to take off from JFK I met him and his parents in New York and we all went to the airport together and, amid much weeping, he left. His parents had arranged for me to stay in a hotel on Central Park South that night. It was very fancy.

The next morning we got up, had a nice breakfast and they returned to Buffalo while I took the train back to my parents' house. I'd been there about two hours when the phone rang. It was Nelson. He was back in New York. His plane had landed in Belgium and it was raining so he came home. My year hiatus before getting married had just been cancelled. Suddenly he was in a rush. He seemed to think I'd get pregnant immediately and would be his ticket out of the draft. I didn't want to marry him but went ahead with it because if he got drafted I'd feel it was all my fault and in all honesty I didn't know what else to do.

It was a small wedding by choice at a Justice of the Peace. My honeymoon was one night at the Holiday Inn in Binghamton, New York after which we continued to Buffalo where Nelson had a job as a ski instructor for the winter. I realized I had made a huge mistake when, once in the hotel room, I tried to surprise him with a bottle of champagne I had in my bag. When he saw me try to open it he said "What are you doing? We should save that for a special occasion!"

The marriage went downhill quickly. We lived in a tiny cinderblock summer cottage that was insufficiently heated for winter in the mountains south of Buffalo. I spent about four hours a day trying to dig my car out of the snow after the plow came through. I caught rheumatic fever. Nelson came home drunk most nights and was sometimes physically abusive. He was unfaithful. Going to Vietnam wouldn't have been an ethical problem for Nelson. It would have been just a big inconvenience. Worried for his son, his father arranged for their neighbor, the family doctor, to tell the draft board that Nelson had flat feet. Of all the boys I knew who had tried one way or another to keep from being forced to fight a war they didn't believe in, Nelson is the only one who seems to me to have been dishonorable. With no moral compass of his own his father had taken care of it for him. And after he was 4F he realized he didn't need me anymore.

We stuck it out through that winter and then when summer came moved to Phoenix where he was to attend graduate school. Another cinderblock cottage, this one with no air conditioning. It was all too much and when he said he wanted out I was glad. I drove back east, found a job, an apartment and got on with my life.

***

When Terry asked me to write a chapter for this book I couldn't think of what I could contribute. By the sheer luck of being born female I didn't go to Vietnam. I never had to fight. My life wasn't in danger. The more I thought about it though, I realized how Vietnam did affect my life, and that of everyone else I knew, in one way or another. I hated the war and what it did to the boys who fought there, who we lost and what it did to the country. It screwed up my life in ways I never could have foreseen and it took a long time for me to unscrew it. Marriage never crossed my mind again.

I was comfortably tucked in my own little government-subsidized apartment celebrating by myself when Richard Nixon resigned and that signified the end of the whole Vietnam era for me. Unfortunately though, over the years, I have sadly come to realize that there will always be another war and there will always be another generation to send into battle.

CITIZEN SOLDIER – Don Bentivoglio dropped out of college in 1967 and became an infantry officer in the Army, serving in the Vietnam War and bringing many memories and lessons home. (Photo courtesy of Don Bentivoglio)

CHAPTER SIX
Strange Year in a Young Man's Life

BY DON BENTIVOGLIO

My story isn't a whole lot different than most of the stories of the roughly three million military personnel who served on active duty during the Vietnam War. Most of us would have preferred to have been somewhere else, but one way or the other we were called to service, we showed up and we did our very best at a very young age.

For me, an unusual three-plus year period of my life started in May of 1968 when I received my "invitation" (aka draft notice) from President Johnson to join the armed services.

Those who were drafted from Lower Bucks County remember the drill. An early morning appointment with the Draft Board in Bristol Borough followed by a bus ride to 401 North Broad Street for our physical examination.

Soon after the examination I received the inevitable letter telling me when to report back to the Induction Center to be sent to a designated training center. My next step took me to Fort Bragg, North Carolina. Eight weeks at Fort Bragg and then on to beautiful Fort Dix for another eight weeks of advanced individual training (AIT).

I was accepted to Officer Candidate School (OCS) and received orders to report to Fort Benning, GA for 20-plus weeks of intense training and instruction on leadership techniques, problem solving and infantry tactics. While in OCS I was introduced to the idea of jumping out of planes (the thought of an extra $110 a month probably didn't hurt) and the idea of Ranger School also intrigued me. I was accepted at both and graduated as a Second Lieutenant Airborne Ranger. Quite a leap considering less than a year earlier I was working as a steelworker at Fairless Works in Morrisville, PA.

I was subsequently assigned to the 82nd Airborne Division back at Fort Bragg where my Army journey began. I had some really cool jobs in the 82nd and was able to attend a couple more specialized schools while jumping until my heart's content. The inevitable finally visited and I received my orders to Vietnam.

I don't really remember how, but somehow, I made my way to the Philadelphia Airport for a flight to the Seattle/Tacoma airport where I boarded Flying Tiger Airlines which graciously transported me to the Cam Ranh Bay Base Camp in the sunny Republic of Vietnam. I remember taxiing to a stop where a young Sergeant boarded the aircraft to "welcome" us to Vietnam and to give an overview of the next 24 to 48 hours. Among procedural issues, his spiel included where the pool was, how to get to the beach and where the basketball courts were. I remember thinking that I must have missed the memo about the war coming to an end because I was expecting mortars and bullets coming our way. Once we were off the plane we were assigned a bed in a "replacement" barracks to await reassignment. I had no sooner unpacked my duffle bag when an officious Specialist came into the barracks and shouted my name. I acknowledged that I was there and was told that I had 30 minutes to get back to the runway to board my next flight to my initial duty station. I do remember wondering "what happened to my 24 to 48 hours of the beach, pool and basketball courts."

The flight to my initial station was about 45 minutes or so in a Caribou transport plane. For the newly initiated, these planes shook like hell when the engines were running at full blast and it wasn't a warm feeling as they took off, flew and landed. Luckily, I had experience jumping out of them while with the 82nd Airborne Division and had confidence in their ability to stay aloft. We landed in Nha Trang, the back ramp opened, and the Crew Chief encouraged us to quickly exit the aircraft. I was met by a jeep driver who took me to the detachment area where I was to meet my next bosses. I believe that the feeling as a relatively new Second Lieutenant still in rumpled class A's walking among highly experienced (and generally laughing and snickering) field troops is akin to being the only naked mummer prancing down Broad Street in Philadelphia on New Year's Day.

My permanent duty station was changed after a month or so because the detachment was essentially dissolved and reallocated. I received orders for the 25th Infantry Division in Cu Chi (III Corps) which didn't please me as it wasn't an airborne unit and, among other things, I lost my $110 per month jump pay which was roughly 15 percent of my monthly pay. Back to a landing pad for a flight to Cu Chi where I was introduced to the Battalion Commander of the 2/27 Infantry Regiment (Wolfhounds) and was assigned to my new platoon. It was here that my Vietnam experience really started.

I was assigned to D Company and introduced to my new platoon, which consisted of soldiers mostly my age who obviously had far more in-country experience. It was harder winning over your new platoon in Vietnam than it was in the states because these guys knew they were expected to put their lives in your hands. In stateside duty, the platoon just had to put up with you, hope that you weren't a jerk and that you somewhat knew what you were doing.

In Vietnam, a new officer had to quickly convince his soldiers that he did know what he was doing. If you failed at convincing them, life in a combat zone would really suck. As it turned out, I was handed a great group of guys who were highly experienced, but still willing to accept my lack of combat experience until I proved myself. Fortunately, I had some outstanding senior NCO's in the 82nd who had schooled me in the idea that it is the NCO's who can either make your life miserable or be a big part of the reason for your success.

For my first couple of reconnaissance and ambush patrols, I let the platoon sergeant or squad leaders continue to lead our patrols so I could see how they did things in order to learn what they were doing well and whether or not I could improve on their tactics. I believe that this small consideration helped with their acceptance of me as their "leader."

We've all read about individual experiences as a combat troop in Vietnam and the stories have been told over and over. Many of the experiences were horrifying and life-changing when you were in a firefight, or otherwise engaged with the enemy. It is during these situations that your instincts and training took over and you truly appreciated those who are around you as you are quickly reinforced with the idea that you have to depend on each other to get you through the situation.

This dependence goes well beyond those to your immediate right and left. You had to trust in a series of people: that whoever called in coordinates for supporting artillery fire knew what they are doing; that the artillery batteries (who you would never meet in person) were expected to put the rounds on target and not on top of you; the gunship pilots who were supporting you during the action; the Air Force and Navy pilots who were delivering the 360 degrees of napalm and other ordinance to suppress the enemy; and eventually the chopper pilots who either came to resupply you, to extract your team (often from a "hot" landing zone) or to evacuate the dead and wounded.

I didn't necessarily understand it at the time, but as an infantry grunt I often felt that we were at the bottom of the proverbial food chain. In retrospect I actually had multi-million dollars' worth of supporting lethal assets at my fingertips and generally available whenever needed. If all else failed, there was often the Battalion Commander flying a Command and Control (C&C) chopper above you assisting in getting you whatever support you needed. Looking back, it was pretty heady stuff for a 22-year-old who had just passed the minimum age to be able to buy a drink in the States a year or two previously.

Combat in Vietnam was often the proverbial periods of absolute adrenalin-hyped terror interspersed with periods of boredom when you walked for clicks (map terminology for 1,000 meters) in rice paddies and jungles looking for anything of interest or sat on an ambush trail all day or night hoping that some unsuspecting enemy would wander past. It is during these "boring" periods when you had to ensure that you didn't let your guard down.

Bouncing around the jungles in III Corps kept life interesting and exciting enough for all of us, but in late April of 1970, President Nixon decided that it was important to invade the Parrot's Beak region of Cambodia to interdict the Ho Chi Minh Trail (which was probably the most bombed trail in history) and to find the headquarters of the NVA's Central Office for South Vietnam (COSVN). My unit had been dispatched (often hurriedly) a number of times previously in Vietnam whenever we received intel that COSVN was "located," but we were usually late and generally just ran into stragglers (whose main purpose in life was to make our life miserable) and base camps that had been recently evacuated.

Our incursion into Cambodia yielded generally the same results. We found some large caches of supplies, some recently emptied base camps, bothersome snipers and a number of squads of NVA ... but never the elusive COSVN. As part of the dark humor of infantry grunts, I remember thinking that the Army didn't think they screwed with us enough by sending us to Vietnam, they felt they had to up their game by sending us to Cambodia. The good news was that the Cambodian jungles didn't look much different than the Vietnamese jungles, so we were able to perform at the same high level that we did in Vietnam. My teams were good in the jungle, so it really didn't matter which jungle we were in. After a couple of weeks in Cambodia, we were sent "home" to Vietnam. Who knew that we would ever view Vietnam as home?

After 40 years or so of retrospection, there are things that stand out in my mind. First and foremost are the team members who were killed or seriously wounded. I will never forget their names. Whenever I read books or articles about Vietnam, I remember them like it was yesterday. The second most vivid memory is the camaraderie of the most disparate group of guys that I had ever been associated with up until that time. We came from all parts of the US, had wildly different backgrounds, were of a number of ethnic and racial backgrounds and often had totally different social and political views. The proverbial glue that held us together in the field was that we needed and depended on each other to survive. To most of us, that's the only thing that mattered. On the rare times we returned to Cu Chi base camp to reequip, rearm and to stand down for a couple of days, many of the guys would generally hang with their own groups and do their own thing, but back in the field we were once again a cohesive team.

You shared experiences with these individuals that you couldn't (or wouldn't) share with family or those who weren't in Vietnam. I kept up with a number of colleagues over the years after my service, but over time we went about our separate lives. Recently, and totally unexpectedly, I reconnected with three former Platoon Members: Wayne Schoof (one of my Platoon Sergeants); Dave Shepard, one of our machine gunners; and Phil Jacques, our Platoon Medic. We've shared some pictures that we still have and have corresponded via email.

It's interesting that with each email exchange, memories long forgotten come to mind as you start exchanging the inevitable "have you ever heard from" questions. Because I was one of the fortunate ones who returned relatively unscathed, most of my memories are favorable. The Army (including VN) was a life-defining experience that proved who you were deep inside, what you are capable of doing when under extreme pressure and how important those around you are when you need them and they need you. These lessons served us throughout our various careers.

I started this chapter by saying I now realize that I was not all that special. I was one of close to three million GI's who served on active duty during our involvement in the war and simply came home and resumed our lives where we left off. I was fortunate to have received excellent training by highly dedicated career officers and NCO's, to have served with and to be mentored by the same types of people and to have come in contact with some of the best 20-year-old guys that this country had to offer. The veterans of WWII are deservedly called "The Greatest Generation," but I would submit that we didn't do too bad ourselves. Our recognition came late, but I believe we are better understood and appreciated now than ever before.

LASTING TREASURE – The people of Pawtucket, R.I. raised $40,000 and dedicated this monument in 2017 to the 21 former city residents who died in the Vietnam War. (Photo courtesy of Terry Nau)

CHAPTER SEVEN
Pawtucket Remembers

BY TERRY NAU

Sometimes a book project takes on a life of its own. That's what happened to me in 2015-16 when I began researching, interviewing and writing my book about Pawtucket's 21 Vietnam War casualties. The project became a series of interlinked pieces of karma that led me into the heart of a city that I really did not know at all, even after 34 years of living and working within the community as sports editor of the *Pawtucket Times*.

A previous book of mine dealt with the 15 KIAs from my high school alma mater back in Pennsylvania, where I lived for the first 35 years of my life, minus two in the Army. When the book, "*We Walked Right Into It*," came out in 2015, my girlfriend, Cheryl Britland, said, "You've lived in Pawtucket half of your life. You have to write the same book about the place where you live. This is your home."

Home is a funny word. When people would ask me where I am "from," I usually told them Pennsylvania, because I was born in Pittsburgh and grew up in the suburbs of Philadelphia. I knew just about every street and neighborhood in my little hometown of Fairless Hills. It was hard for me to say the same thing about Pawtucket. I can still draw a blank when natives talk about a certain street or neighborhood. If you don't grow up in a place, you can't call it home. Or at least that was my opinion.

Cheryl was right, of course. So I looked up the list of Vietnam War casualties from Pawtucket and learned there were 20 KIAs. I would add one more, Albert Haslam, during my book research, when a local Vietnam veteran named Bill Donnelly told me Albert lived the last two years of his civilian life in Pawtucket before he was inducted into the Army. That was good enough for me, even though the Army listed Albert's hometown as Central Falls, the next town over.

My first order of business was to establish a Facebook page as base of operations. I needed help from Pawtucket residents who could steer me to families of those 21 soldiers. In my prior book, finding families was not a problem because I grew up in that community and personally knew some of the soldiers who died, or knew how to find their family and friends. But Pawtucket was a different story. I had no lay of the land, very little idea about the various neighborhoods, or the parishes, which I came to learn are just as important. Pawtucket is, like, 70 percent Catholic. Kids grew up in St. Teresa's parish, or St. Leo's. That's how friends distinguished their neighborhoods.

After stating my purpose on the Facebook page, a local veteran named Jim Raftus got in touch with an old friend, Steve Eno, who had served in Vietnam. I found this out later. But one day, my phone rang, and Steve Eno asked if I wanted to meet at his office and talk about my book project. Turns out, Steve had served in my old artillery outfit, about one year after I left Vietnam in 1968. So we made a connection.

"I was just trying to find out if you were legit," Steve told me a year later, after the book, *"They Heard the Bugle's Call,"* came out.

Steve graduated from St. Raphael Academy in 1964 along with two of the 21 Heroes, Jack Hulme and Michael Dalton. He put me in touch with Michael's sister Mary, and that's when my research began to gain momentum.

Mary invited me to meet at her home over near Brown University in Providence. I walked in to find Mary and her sister June waiting with some trepidation, as Michael's death had impacted their family in a deep way, and still resonated with them 44 years later. I was ill-prepared to sit down and get to know them right away. I just had a list of questions that I ran through. The interview might have lasted 45 minutes and then I was gone. It's just the way I work. Old newspapermen are always in a rush because there is usually a deadline to meet.

I had set a deadline of getting this book published before the 50th anniversary of the city's first casualty, Marine Corporal Antonio Maciminio Jr., who had died on May 21, 1966. I wanted my book done and in print by May 2016. That would be eight months from the beginning of my research. You can work fast when you self-publish. Pay your own way. No editors or book agents to slow things down. I had a deadline, just like in my newspaper career.

I just kept lining up interviews, with my Facebook friends providing tips along the way. I struck up a friendship by phone and email with Cathy Maciminio Dumont, who had married Tony Maciminio in August 1965 and was the mother of his only child, Vicky. Mother and daughter both lived in Florida now but were so honest and kind to me, I felt like I knew them. A wedding photo of Cathy revealed a beautiful young girl, smiling and happy, posing with her husband, nine months before his death.

HAPPY COUPLE – Tony Maciminio and his wife Cathy were married in August 1965, less than a year before he would die in the Vietnam War. Cathy gave birth to their only child, Vicky, in October 1966. (Photo courtesy of Cathy Dumont)

A key part of my research began in November 2015 when I went up to the fourth floor of my old newspaper, the *Pawtucket Times*, and began looking through back issues from 1966-71, searching for the stories of these soldiers' deaths. The *Times* had moved most of its employees to Woonsocket by then, and only three people remained on the first floor. I would be all alone on the fourth floor, pulling heavy newspaper-sized books off shelves, each bound according to months of the year. There were no distractions. And I began tracking down the stories, coming a few days after soldiers' deaths, often with a bylined story and photos of their funerals a few days later. The early deaths drew a lot of attention, as the war sneaked up on the city's citizens in 1966 and 1967.

The *Times* tended to play things straight, covering the wider war with wire stories and photographs, occasionally lambasting the "hippies and protestors" on its editorial page. But by the time of the fourth death in October 1967 -- Marine Lt. Charles Yaghoobian Jr. -- the editorial page noted that the true cost of the war might be measured in the loss of a city's young citizens, the leaders of tomorrow. Charles Yaghoobian was one such man, a teacher in local schools who had taken ROTC in college at the University of Rhode Island, back when ROTC was mandatory. He was activated by the Marine Corps in April 1967, and arrived in Vietnam on Oct. 12. The son of an Armenian restauranteur was airlifted to his new unit two days later, at a combat base near the DMZ called Con Thien, which had been under siege for months. The base was overrun that night and Charles Yaghoobian, on his first day with his unit, was among 21 KIA and 23 wounded in that massacre.

The *Times*, whose employees were all familiar with the Yaghoobian's family restaurant, located 200 yards down the hill from its office on Exchange Street, wrote an editorial not long after Charlie's funeral:

"The costs of war are horrible and varied – the lives that can never be replaced and the heartbreak of loved ones ... the dollar costs of the lethal weapons man uses to settle disputes. But there's another – the loss, in this instance, that Pawtucket has suffered. A young man who sought nothing more than to play a role in fashioning the community's greatest asset – its young people. Lt. Yaghoobian is the fourth young man whose talents have been lost to Pawtucket in the Vietnam War. And what is happening to Pawtucket is happening to thousands

of other communities from coast to coast. Not all of war's costs carry dollar signs."

Sitting in a dusty room on the second floor, I winced at these words, and speculated about how the war must have been changing the newsroom at the *Times* in the 1960s. I know how a newspaper office works, having started in the business for real in 1972. Older editors set in their ways. Young reporters trying to change the world with every bylined story. Old and young clashing over an unpopular war, not only in newspaper offices but in the streets across our country, as good men died 10,000 miles from home.

That editorial really made me start thinking of Pawtucket as it existed during the war. I had arrived in Vietnam six weeks before Charlie Yaghoobian. So I had a timeline now, a frame of reference, and I started to live these stories, especially after I met some of the families. Charlie had two sisters, Nathalie and Zita, who were very protective of their brother's memory when I interviewed them, and so proud. Their church had perpetuated a scholarship in his memory over the past four decades. So did his college. It was said that Charlie seemed to know everyone, and everyone knew him.

I started to expand my research, layer by layer. Mary Dalton and I became pals, mostly by email, and she arranged a phone call with her brother Michael's widow, Debbie, who had delivered a son, Scott, three months before her husband died. Debbie eventually moved to the west coast to get away from the pain that clung to her in Pawtucket and her home state, New Jersey. She married again and had two more children. In recent years, Debbie has begun bringing Scott's children to Rhode Island each summer to stay with Mary and June down at the beach.

During my book research, though it was a very painful process, Debbie began to help me paint a fuller picture of her first husband, her first love, and as she told me, "Just know that there is no love like your first love. Michael was my first love. I still have dreams of him."

Jack Hulme came alive to me in a film documentary produced by his son, John IV, and shown on HBO in 2005. Jack was a football star in high school and college, where he played quarterback for the University of Bridgeport. During that blissful time frame, he fell in love and married a girl from New Jersey, Ellen Bratter. Jack was also infatuated with the Marine Corps, or at least he was until love softened his outlook on life and made him a more centered person.

Still, the Marine Corps commitment persisted. At his graduation ceremony, Jack proudly wore his dress white Marine Corps uniform, and when it came time for him to accept his diploma, some professors and students got up and walked out. This was 1968, in Connecticut. The Vietnam War had already bottomed out at home in America, especially on the more progressive college campuses.

I came home from the war in September 1968 and enrolled at a Penn State branch campus just outside of Philadelphia. We veterans learned quickly not to speak about the war -- not that I was inclined to do so anyway. The students in my classes were 18 or 19 years old, mostly against the war unless they had a brother in uniform, and even then, the war was too easy a target. I came home thinking we were losing the war and our country, too. So why bring it up with anyone who did not understand the true cost of war, the lives of those American soldiers, many of them the same age as these college students? I got through college by forgetting about Vietnam and focusing on my life, burying my own memories of war for the next 35 years.

One night in January 2016, during a lull in my book research, *The Times* assigned me to cover a high school basketball game at St. Raphael Academy, alma mater of Michael Dalton and Jack Hulme. I had covered many games at SRA over the years but this one was different. Their stories of these two alumni were now a part of me. I arrived early, walked down Walcott Street and looked at the street plaque honoring Michael that hung from a 10-foot pole. I had never noticed it before, not in 30 years and many prior visits to this campus. And then I went inside the gym, a shiny new building bearing no resemblance to the cramped gymnasium that Jack and Mike played in. I sat high in the bleachers and played games in my head, thinking they were sitting with me, talking about how much their school had changed since they were teenagers.

Yes, this story was getting personal, almost spiritual. And I had no idea how rewarding the journey would become over the next two years.

The book came out in April. I rushed it through in five months. Self-published. Paid for it myself because waiting for a literary agent to find a publisher would have extended the process by years. I long ago had reconciled the fact that my writing is succinct but never spellbinding. I write like a newspaper guy. Get to the point! So five months is not a big deal to me. Hell, we wrote 800-word stories in 45 minutes on deadline, not just me but almost everyone in a good newsroom. It's just the nature of the beast. Even Mary Dalton understood after a while that I was in a perpetual rush.

When the books arrived at my house, I took one over to Mary.

"We have to have a book signing," she said, being nice, and suggested her husband's law office on Newport Avenue, a venue that might hold 30 people at one time. Within a week, we knew we needed a larger place to host our event, because the initial response suggested maybe 100 people. So we asked the city of Pawtucket and they agreed to lend us the use of a new outdoor venue in Slater Park, the Pavilion, which might accommodate 150 people.

We publicized the event on Facebook. Cathy Dumont and her daughter Vicky announced they were flying up from Florida. Debbie Dalton was coming in from San Francisco. That's when Mary and I realized we needed to do a proper ceremony. We asked City Council to proclaim May 21 as "21 Heroes Day." And they did.

On monument dedication day, people began arriving 90 minutes before the ceremony was scheduled to begin. Some of the veterans just wanted to talk. Mike Costigan came over to me. I knew his brother Greg but had only heard of Mike, a Vietnam veteran, an infantryman. And Mike started telling me how he caught a touchdown pass in 1962 from Michael Dalton that beat Bishop Hendricken. I told him to tell Mary, and she heard the story for the first time. Mary had been a little girl who sometimes rode on her big brother's shoulders on the way to the game, when the players walked to the gridiron.

We had nearly 200 people in attendance, most of them products of the 1950s and 1960s, people who had grown up with at least one of the 21 Heroes. Thirteen of the 21 Gold Star families were represented, and they each spoke at the microphone in emotional terms about their soldier. Tears flowed all over The Pavilion. Sue Geary

Turnquist spoke for her high school classmate Johnny Maloney, recalling how she heard he had been killed in the war while driving in her car on I-95. She heard this news on the radio and had to pull off the road, where she began sobbing.

Debbie Dalton closed the ceremony with these words:

"My husband, Michael Dalton, died on June 9, 1971, nine weeks after our son, Scott, was born. Michael was the last soldier from Pawtucket to die in Vietnam. There is no special glory in being the first of the 21 or the last. Our stories are all different, some more similar than others, but we are connected always by having lost someone we deeply loved, still dream of and forever yearn for, whose legacies carry their names, their smiles and their spirit."

After the ceremony ended, one of my Pawtucket friends, Greg Murphy, approached. His father, Jim Murphy, had been at editor at *The Times* back in the 1960s and 1970s. Greg grew up in that era so he knew some of the 21.

"This crowd here today," he said, "this is Old Pawtucket."

Most of that crowd had moved away, some to the suburbs, some to Providence, others to warmer climes, but this event had drawn them back home to honor their fallen friends.

You would think that is the end of the story. I thought so. So did Mary. And then it dawned on us that we needed a monument to honor the heroes. Paul Renaud planted the idea when he told me his brother Robert, who died in the war just two weeks after his 19th birthday, had never been honored by the city with a street plaque. Further research showed that only 15 had been honored. Something had to be done. We needed one substantial monument that would list all 21 names.

Back to the Facebook page. We started a non-profit called 21 Heroes Inc, and began raising money. Those people from Old Pawtucket responded. The widow of former Pawtucket Red Sox owner Ben Mondor donated $5,000 in his memory. Former Hasbro owner Allen Hassenfeld donated $2,000. Several companies pitched in. I threw in $1,000 from book proceeds. City Safety Director Tony Pires, who knew Charles Yaghoobian, donated $1,000 in his memory. Donations from the Gold Star families accounted for nearly $14,000. My barber,

John Petteruti, a Vietnam War infantryman, raised over $3,000 from his customers. Three anonymous Vietnam veterans donated over $200. One Vietnam vet, Joe Marques, went around town and collected nearly $1,000 in donations. The checks just kept rolling in to our post office box and by November we had accumulated nearly $40,000.

We found a monument company in nearby Cranston through a connection with 21 Heroes. The monument company owner, Anthony Sciolto, was a cousin of a fallen Pawtucket hero, Valentino La Scola. The Scioltos accepted the job without hesitation and promised it would be done by the following May. Anthony's son, Tony, a Vietnam Era veteran, designed the monument for us on the back of a piece of paper, and delivered on his design, and his promise, by early May 2017.

The monument, eight feet wide and six feet high, featured a centerpiece of black African stone, just like The Wall in Washington, D.C. Across the top were the words, "Pawtucket's 21 Vietnam War Heroes." Anthony Sciolto, just three weeks shy of his 100th birthday, drove the forklift on May 6 while his son Tony called out instructions as the monument was installed, in plenty of time for our ceremony.

This time, we had nearly 600 people in attendance on the edge of Slater Park, where the monument rests of a grassy knoll, overlooking Armistice Boulevard. A two-star Marine Corps General from Pawtucket, John Broadmeadow, delivered the keynote address, telling the audience that "These soldiers were not honored properly when they came home from Vietnam. What we are doing here today is remembering the dedication and service of these 21 young men who sacrificed their lives for their country, and for each other."

The monument has been well-received in the community, quickly becoming a place of interest, especially for people of a certain age. Vietnam veterans have been known to stop by and pay their respects. Students from Goff Junior High lay Christmas wreaths at the monument each December. Gold Star families finally feel like they have a place to come and reflect. Mary Dalton stops by from time to time to spruce up the plant holder at the base of the monument. A Vietnam vet, Bob Lincourt, maintains the grass around the monument, all on his own, without any fanfare.

So this is how a city remembers the 21 former residents who were killed in action in the Vietnam War. And for me, the whole experience of writing a book, and seeing a city respond to our monument fundraising drive, revealed the heart of the place I moved to in 1982. When people now ask me where I am from, I tell them "Pawtucket, Rhode Island."

LEGACY – Michael Dalton's grandson, also named Michael, spoke his grandfather's name as his grandmother, Debbie, looked on during 21 Heroes monument dedication ceremony in 2017. (Photo courtesy of Dana Siles)

MONUMENTAL – Jim Raftus, in the back row, looms over the 21 Heroes committee, nicknamed the Loose Cannons after a popular craft beer. Jim found
great meaning in the experience of creating a monument dedicated to soldiers
from his hometown. (Photo courtesy of Terry Nau)

CHAPTER EIGHT
A Reluctant Soldier's Story

BY JIM RAFTUS

SEPTEMBER 1966
I DODGE THE DRAFT. BY ACCIDENT.

It didn't take very long for the local draft board to discover I had spent far too much time on the basketball court and the student center at Rhode Island College and not enough time in the classrooms. By the end of my freshman year I'd essentially dropped out of school. My draft notice arrived in early summer. I dutifully went to my physical and was declared 1-A. In September my notification to report for duty had arrived. I was the first of my peers to be drafted. My friends gave me a grand going-away party. They rented adjoining rooms at the local Holiday Inn and packed the place to say "goodbye." I recall great quantities of beer flowing amidst the strange mix of hilarity and sadness. The reality of Vietnam had entered our complacent world.

The following morning my father drove me to the Army's Fields Point disembarkment facility in Providence. A normally stoic man, he teared up as I got out of the car. A fairly large contingent of young men quietly filled out the necessary paperwork before the swearing in ceremony. We would then proceed to board the trains which would transport us to our basic training forts scattered up and down the eastern seaboard.

"Raftus, is there a James Raftus here?" a voice called out above the quiet conversations.

I meekly raised my hand.

"Follow me," ordered the uniformed young man.

He led me to a side room and told me to wait. I was the only future soldier singled out. I was confused. A few minutes passed before a doctor entered. My confusion increased. This was not a day for physicals, this was the day all the young men in the adjoining room would be placing their fates in the hands of the United States Army that was involved in an increasingly bloody war.

The doctor examined me, then announced that I had a heretofore undiagnosed physical problem and that he was declaring me 4-F unfit for duty. The problem, he explained, was neither life-threatening nor did it require surgery but still made me exempt from serving. I did not argue with the doctor's decision.

I took the going away money my father had given me and hired a taxi to take me to my girlfriend's home in Pawtucket. I had last seen her the night before at my party. She was shocked and amazed when I showed up at her door. In hindsight, while she was happy she did not seem as ecstatic as I expected. Four months later we broke up.

MARCH 1968
THE ARMY CHANGES ITS MIND

The number of American troops deployed to Vietnam in 1965 was 184,300. In 1967 it had swelled to 485,600. The number of U.S. casualties between my first draft notice in September of 1966 and the Spring of 1968 was approximately 18,000 and nearly 100,000 had been wounded.

Uncle Sam decided to take another look at James Raftus. The notice I received for a new medical examination included the instructions to bring proof of any prior physical exemptions to this new appointment. So, I obligingly brought my previous 4-F status to the new exam. After a quick look the doctor decided my issue, which the other doctor had discovered in 1966, was not a disqualifying problem and I was immediately reclassified as 1-A.

Vietnam was now a daily newspaper front page issue. The Tet offensive in February took a major toll on troops. President Lyndon Johnson had dropped out of his re-election bid on March 31st. On April 4th Martin Luther King was assassinated. The world was in turmoil and I had decisions to make. I knew my draft notice was imminent.

What were my options? Fleeing to Canada was never a consideration, so, instead I opted to enlist rather than be drafted. My rationale, seconded by a recruitment officer, was that while enlisting would mean a three-year commitment versus the two years served by draftees, it would at least allow me to choose my category of job, or military occupation specialty (MOS). I had recently earned a computer programming certificate from a government-sponsored program held at Providence College. I figured this MOS was probably safer than most.

APRIL 25 - SEPTEMBER 22, 1968
BASIC & ADVANCED INDIVIDUAL TRAINING

This time there was no last-second reprieve. I was sworn in as an enlisted man at Fields Point and boarded a train which took this reluctant soldier to basic training at Fort Jackson in Columbia, South Carolina. It was my first venture into the Deep South. There was one other Rhode Islander with me as we arrived and entered our new home, the two-level barracks. After the obligatory shouting and harassment from our drill sergeants, my fellow Rhode Islander and I were kibitzing downstairs when a voice from above called out, "Hey, Irish! Who's that Irish guy down there?" The unseen questioner turned out to be one of a group of New York City black recruits who had settled in together on the second floor. My accent amused them and for the next eight weeks my nickname was "Irish."

It is often said that the military is a great equalizer bringing races together. I would say this was only partially true. It was true that because of simple demographics I'd not socialized with many blacks in Rhode Island. Now for three years I would be part of a racially mixed community. Yet a form of self-segregation often occurred.

I got along well with most everyone, but, tensions were never far below the surface. Oddly my best friend in basic had the darkest skin I have ever seen. His name was Moses McCutcheon and his family worked a small cotton farm only about 30 miles from the fort. He missed his family and knew they needed him on the farm. The temptation for him to go AWOL so close to home was tremendous. With my Rhode Island accent and fast paced delivery and Moses' low, slow southern drawl I'm not sure how we even communicated, but we became good friends. Eventually the New York City blacks confronted Moses, questioning why he was hanging around with this white Irish guy.

This was a big mistake on their part. While Moses was short, about 5'6" compared to my 6'4," he was hardened by years of long, long days of toiling in the fields. Makes a young man stronger than almost anything a city dweller might do. Moses chose one of the larger, loudest of the crew harassing him and swiftly lifted him, pinned the culprit against a metal locker while hissing, "No one is going to tell me who to be friends with!"

The harassment stopped. I completed the long eight weeks military indoctrination period that was meant to strip as much individuality from each soldier as possible and replace it with a commitment to the unit's common good.

Next stop was Fort Lee in Virginia for my eight weeks of Advanced Individual Training (AIT) to turn my computer skills into my military job. This training was in fact a mix of more physical training and class time learning the ins and outs of the military parts supply chain.

What it really felt like was a holding pen leading up to the biggest question of all for everyone involved. Where would we be sent for our permanent duty? When "posting" day arrived we all ran to the bulletin boards where assignments were listed. In an agonizing twist, names were not listed in alphabetical order but randomly. The only obvious thing was that for the first page and a half every name had the initials RVN listed next to them. Republic of Vietnam. Finally halfway down the second page I found my name. Next to my name were two letters AK.

"Arkansas," I thought. "Why would they send me there?"

More significant, of course, was the fact that my name was the first on the list which did not send the reader to Vietnam. Beneath my name there were several other soldiers who had been posted to places such as; Germany, Japan and Korea. After this short break the RVN designations again rolled out. Approximately 75% of my AIT class were headed to a war zone.

In 1968 the U.S. troop numbers peaked at 549,500 and the deaths totaled 16,592.

I silently felt relief tinged with guilt at my assignment.

OCTOBER 1968
THE BIG CHILL

Turns out I was wrong. AK was not Arkansas, but a far more exotic location, Alaska.

The first time I flew from Seattle to my destination, Fort Richardson in Anchorage, I was stunned by the endless snow covered peaks of northwestern Canada. I had never seen such breathtakingly dramatic isolation. On one of the first days of my assignment with the 172nd Infantry Brigade, I was sent to my unit captain's office for an orientation session.

"Do you know why we are here, Specialist Raftus?"

Assuming this was a rhetorical question I simply replied, "No, Sir."

"We are here in case the big balloon goes up," he intoned.

The big balloon was military speak for a nuclear explosion.

"If it goes up, Specialist, do you know the closest place to America that the Russians have infantry?"

I politely demurred.

"In Siberia right across the Bering Straits, young man. That's where they are. And if the Rooskies (he actually said that) try to cross over we'll be here to stop them."

I remembered as a 12-year-old hearing Nikita Khrushchev declaring, "We will bury you!" in what was a financial taunt to capitalistic state leaders. Plus in 1968 we were only six years removed from the frightening nuclear staredown with Russia during the Cuban missile crisis. The cold war was still in full bloom, but the concept of Russia invading Alaska seemed like a subplot from the 1966 comedy farce movie, "The Russians are Coming! The Russians are Coming!"

Probably because I had some college and was a couple of years older than most of the troops I was quickly promoted to Specialist 5th Class and made a squad leader. It certainly was not because I was the most spit and polished dedicated soldier in our group. Fortunately our unit was in charge of vehicle supply parts and was more warehouse and inventory focused than combat trained.

One benefit of my rank was that I was given a room in the barracks rather than living in the shared open space. Occasionally I'd invite the squad in for a bull session while we listened to my vinyl album collection.

One night after I played a stretch which included; Tom Paxton, Bob Dylan, Buffy St. Marie and Phil Ochs, a private from Little Rock, Arkansas named E.Q. Smith looked over at me and drawled, "You know what y'all are Raftus? Y'all a short-haired hippy."

He was near the truth. I doubt many Army barracks had Dylan's "Masters of War" echoing off the walls.

APRIL 1970
TWO FLIGHTS AND A DOSE OF REALITY

Surprisingly the topic of Vietnam rarely surfaced during my first two years in the Army. Even the military "lifers," the Staff Sergeants who were our day to day bosses and had previously served there never talked to us about it. It was almost as if isolated in Alaska we were in a different Army than the service men and women in Southeast Asia.

In April of 1970 I decided to take my leave time in Japan rather than head back to Rhode Island. The World's Fair was being held in Osaka so I hooked up with two buddies and headed to an adventure in Japan.

The flight over was on a military transport plane. Anchorage was a refueling stop for flights carrying new troops to Vietnam after another stop in Japan. We sat on cushions in the curved fuselage, safety straps draped loosely over our shoulders. The first thing I noticed was how young our fellow passengers were. At 23, I was 4 or 5 years older than most of these soldiers heading to war. It was unnerving. There was quiet chatter and sporadic card playing during the long flight, but mostly the mood was subdued. This was only the mid-point flight to their final destination outside of Saigon. I could only imagine the atmosphere would become darker on the final leg.

After a whirlwind week of fun and mishaps in Tokyo and Osaka my little group boarded a flight back to Anchorage. This time it was on a cherished "Freedom Bird" flight home for troops who had finished, and survived, their year in Vietnam. The plane was a commercial carrier, part of the fleet sometimes contracted by the military to carry personnel. Therefore the standard interior was much cheerier than on our flight to Tokyo and matched the spirit of the returning soldiers. It struck me that although logic would dictate most of the returnees were only a year older than the "cherries" we traveled with on the first flight, they seemed more mature, more adult. Perhaps 12 months in a war zone does that to a young person.

The first loud explosion of applause on this return flight happened when the pilot announced we had entered Alaskan air space. The first step in their journey was complete. Another burst of cheers accompanied the screeching of the plane's wheels as we touched down at Elmendorf Air Force Base the facility next to Fort Richardson. Upon disembarking many of the men bent to kiss the tarmac.

My buddies and I left them to their celebrations as we headed to our comparatively much safer sanctuary at the fort. We went back to our duties with a newer, deeper appreciation of our good fortune.

A SOLDIER AND HIS RIFLE

In 1942 Marine Brigadier General William H. Rupertus wrote the "Riflemen's Creed" which was used in Marine boot camps for decades. In part it says, "My rifle is my best friend. It is my life …"

I was issued a M16 rifle as part of my basic training. I did not like it. I did not like the smell of it. I did not like the heft of it. I did not like the sound of it. I did not like the butt which slammed back into my shoulder in recoil when I fired it.

Because I was a kid who grew up in the suburbs this rifle was the first weapon I had ever held. I knew that in war the rifle was not only part of your own defense but also the protector of your fellow soldiers. But to me in basic training it was just a huge annoyance. Beyond its physical repugnance it was also a constant worry. The drill sergeants aggressively warned all recruits to take 100% care of their rifles. They would scheme and plot ways to separate you from your rifle. If they succeeded the consequences would be dire. I had many wake-inducing nightmares about losing my rifle.

105

Every new soldier had to "qualify" with their rifle on the shooting range. Just about everyone did well enough to earn their first military medal which was a marksmanship badge by hitting at least 23 out of 40 targets. Many recruits did well enough, hitting more than 30, to earn a sharpshooter badge while a few hit at least 36 and were rewarded the coveted expert badge. With my antipathy for shooting I barely passed with 24 hits in basic training.

You needed to re-qualify every two years, so I reluctantly headed back to a rifle range towards the end of my Alaskan tour. But, I had a plan. My best Army friend in Alaska, Gary Smith, was like me a lanky, pale complexioned soldier, but, he loved to hunt and shoot. Each shooter had a spotter kneeling next to their foxhole while they qualified. I was Gary's spotter as he tore up the target sheet earning his expert badge. We then feigned switching places and Gary shot for me. Lo and behold I went from a lowly marksman to an expert without ever having to pull the trigger!

No, the M16 was not my best friend, but Gary Smith was.

WINTER 1969 ALASKA
ON THE ROAD AGAIN - MANEUVERS

Shortly after arriving at Fort Richardson I was told I should get my military jeep operator's license. The test was a simple ten-minute drive around a large, empty parking lot to see if I could handle the jeep's stick shift gears. Because I had owned an old used MG as a civilian, this was no problem. The sergeant administering the test then asked in an off-handed, almost joking way if I wanted to try the shift on a nearby trailer-less cab. As a lark, I said, "Sure." and spent five minutes grinding away at the more complicated 10-gear system of the cab while lurching around the vacant lot.

A few months later our supply group was to be part of the infantry brigades' semi-annual maneuver operation to Fort Wainwright near Fairbanks. The roster of duties was posted. Much to my amazement I had been assigned as a driver of a cab with a fully equipment loaded 18-wheeler with trailer attached. I had not touched a military vehicle since my jeep driving test and now the Army wanted me to drive a full rig on a 360-mile winter trip on the treacherous snow and ice covered Alcan Highway! I raced up the stairs to our Captain's office to straighten out this insanity. My initial arguments fell on deaf ears until I finally put my case in dramatic terms the military man could appreciate.

"You can replace me and the guy riding shotgun, Captain, when we go off the cliff, but you'll have a hard time replacing all those big, expensive computers we're hauling in the trailer!"

I was reassigned to riding shotgun for Corporal Richie Holmein, an experienced, mechanically-inclined driver. Still, the trip was not without incident.

Approximately 150 miles outside of Anchorage our rig started to fail and we were forced to pull to the side of the road and watch the rest of our convoy pass. As the higher-ranking soldier, I radioed the 1st Lieutenant in charge of our platoon. The very short Alaskan winter daylight hours were ending and the frigid temperature continued to plummet. The conversation went like this.

Spec. 5 Raftus -- "Yes, Sir, our driver is a good mechanic but couldn't fix the problem."

1st Lieutenant -- "Well, Specialist, all our tow vehicles are busy. We can't get you until tomorrow."

Spec. 5 Raftus -- "Ok, what are our orders, Sir?"

1st Lieutenant -- "I want you and your driver to take turns doing 20 minutes each, marching around your vehicle while the other stays in the cab."

Spec. 5 Raftus -- "Uh, yes, Sir. Twenty-minute shifts."

By now it was beyond cold with a numbing wind. The truck was going nowhere. The trailer was securely locked. The cab was almost as cold as the outside.

Although stranded in the middle of nowhere, Richie and I remembered seeing a small shack of an office with 3 basic modular units behind it and a "Nightly Rentals" sign hanging out front. It was a make-shift mini-camp for hunters and adventurers to stay overnight and it was only 1/4 mile away. We nodded at each other in tacit agreement and headed down the highway. The rental entrepreneur was happy for the business and we were happy to see that the place also sold essentials including a bottle of Jack Daniels and a deck of cards.

Fortunately the person pounding on our door the following morning, waking us from a groggy somewhat alcohol induced sleep, was a friendly Sergeant who I'd played basketball with back at the fort. He shook his head at us but understood our decision-making process. A crack mechanic and a new battery had us rolling within half an hour and we joined our comrades a day late and a few dollars short.

My two-year stint in Alaska ended and I was sent to Fort Meade in Maryland to finish out my commitment. As tradition for "short timers," I X'd out each remaining day on my wall calendar. I tolerated the billowing pot smoke from my roommate's near constant pipe bowl. Because I had been accepted back into college, I was discharged three months early, having served 33 of my 36 months. I'd noticed other dischargees had filled their duffel bags with as much military gear and memorabilia as they could get away with to bring home. I took a different route. I lined up all my stuff on my bunk bed and left it to be picked over by my last barracks mates.

On January 25th, 1971, keeping only my dress greens which I needed to wear to catch a free flight home, I left the Army behind.

May 21, 2017
CLOSURE

Forty plus years later I have lived a fortunate life. Wonderful wife, great children now adults, delightful grandchildren, nice career and, finally, a comfortable, pleasant retirement. The three-year Army stint seemed an aberration in the normal flow of my life. Despite my reluctance I had done my duty. I only stayed in contact with one other veteran of the 172nd brigade. I thought about my service time more than I spoke about it. When I did think about it I pondered the question of why I wasn't sent to Vietnam and I fought off the guilt which many Vietnam Era veterans who did not serve there feel.

Sometime in 2015 through social media I learned that a gentleman I did not know, Terry Nau, was writing a book about the 21 Pawtucket men who died in Vietnam. Terry, a retired journalist of the *Pawtucket Times* and a Vietnam veteran, was looking for names of Pawtucket veterans who had served there and were willing to tell their stories. I contacted Terry and gave him some names of friends. These men's stories became integral parts of Terry's book "*They Heard the Bugle's Call*." When the book's impact led to the idea of building a Pawtucket's 21 Vietnam Heroes monument, Terry asked me to serve on the committee. I was thrilled to be a small contributor to the process.

On May 21, 2017 the monument ceremony took place at Slater Park in Pawtucket. Three of the 21 men whose names are engraved on the monument were high school classmates of mine. Helping to create this lasting tribute to all the brave young men gave me great solace. I feel less guilty about having served elsewhere. I accept that it was just serendipity which put the letters AK rather than RVN next to my name so many years ago.

Now each Memorial and Veteran's Day this reluctant soldier will join others in reading the names on the monument.

May they rest in peace.

FOR ALL VETERANS – The Vietnam War Memorial in Pawtucket is dedicated to the city's military veterans. Some of them gathered around the monument on Dedication Day in 2017. (Photo courtesy of Terry Nau)

YOUTH FOOTBALL TEAMMATES – Stephen Walach (24) and Bobby Taylor (32) played football and baseball together during the early 1960s before their paths diverged. (Photo courtesy of Stephen Walach)

CHAPTER NINE
Conscientious Objection to War

BY STEPHEN WALACH

After what seemed like an excruciatingly long 1962-1963 school year, June finally rolled in, and for this 14-year-old boy there was no better month. Classes and the torturous homework they inevitably generated were about to disappear just as the baseball season began to heat up. I was graduating as a ninth grader from St. Joseph School on Walcott Street in Pawtucket, less than a mile from my home, and in September I'd be entering St. Raphael Academy, just several blocks on Walcott to the west of St. Joe's — each school very much a part of my extended neighborhood. But high school would have to wait until the Pony League Baseball season ended.

Our team was sponsored by Coats Field — now defunct but one of the original mill textile outlets in the city. Joe Taylor was our coach. Mr. Taylor was one of those many dads from that era who did not advertise themselves as baseball geniuses but who nevertheless gave of their time for the sake of their children and other kids in the city. We benefited by the organization and guiding hand of dedicated adults whether we recognized their selfless service or not.

Mr. Taylor's son Bobby was our gritty shortstop. The shortest guy on the team, Bobby was probably the scrappiest. He made all the routine plays plus some extraordinary ones as well, which made my job as pitcher much easier. Bobby hit from the left side and pumped his bat as he sank deeper into his crouch, making him a tough guy to pitch to. Bobby was a singles hitter and a good bunter. He knew how to work a walk and was never shy about stealing a base.

Even though Bobby lived on the other side of the city in Bishop Bend, we were known to each other. We had competed against each other in Little League and the Pawtucket Boys Club League, a summer morning and afternoon program which was grown-up free. All the teams were organized and managed by kids. No adults. High school ballplayers were the umps. That was a time when we kids worked things out among ourselves and even though we competed hard, I never recall any hard feelings. I sometimes describe the league to my sixth and seventh grade students and they respond with incredulous but envious astonishment. "No adults?" they wistfully ask. Nope, none. Only high school guys who called the ball and strikes. We kids could handle it. I think we were prepared for the responsibility by our no-nonsense parents and also by coaches in the more traditional leagues, whose lessons, examples and expectations gave us knowledge of the game and instilled in us a can-do attitude. In addition, we were used to handling things on our own. That's simply the way it was.

Bobby had also been my teammate on the Darlington Braves, a pre-teen league football team. In 1961, we were league champions for the second consecutive year. Small but determined, Bobby was a defensive stalwart and also played some running back. I played quarterback, and while researching this chapter I came across an eye-opening team picture. Given how events played out, it was an astonishing find. There was Bobby — number 32, sitting to the left of me, number 24. Even while sitting down, he was half a head shorter. Tousle-haired and not in best picturing taking mode, Bobby was absently looking off to his right. We were about to play a crucial game against the Central Falls Townies, and he was probably a bit bored and maybe annoyed as well because Bobby was not one to sit still. I had forgotten about our shared football experience until a vague memory inveigled me to find my old scrapbooks and then pore through them. And there we were, side by side. So close but in the intervening years, so very far apart.

Our Pony League season was no great shakes. We won more often than we lost but overall we had a mediocre season. However, both Bobby and I made the all-star team. But once the season was over I don't believe I ever saw Bobby again, though his father and I met one more time in perhaps the most pivotal moment of my young life.

Later that summer of 1963, I was one of just a couple incoming sophomores invited to catch and throw some passes plus run some plays with Mike Dalton, the presumed starting quarterback for St.

Ray's. Mike was a couple years older than me and was entering his senior year. However, we lived kitty corner across the street and soon after my family had moved into our new home in 1950, I had adopted Mike as my virtual big brother. He more than tolerated my presence, looked out for me, and was always encouraging me sports-wise. Mike did not have to work hard to get me to follow his suggestions. I, along with many in our neighborhood, looked up to — and, you might say, idolized — him as our role model, though we never used or even knew that term. Good-looking, self-assured and loyal, Mike's natural talent for leadership and commitment to the common good made him the perfect best friend, quarterback, and eventually a 1st Lieutenant in the 101st Airborne.

That same languid summer but on the other side of the globe, a stunning, mind-boggling event grabbed the attention of the US media and anyone else who was half paying attention. On June 13th, a day when I was undoubtedly consumed by balls and strikes, hits and home runs, an elderly, Buddhist monk allowed himself to be doused in gasoline. He lit a match, dropped it into his lap, and was engulfed in flames. Vietnam made its jarring debut into the lives of ordinary Americans. More martyred Buddhist monks would follow. And, unfortunately, there was more fire to come from Vietnam, much, much more.

For boys in love with sports and hypnotically immersed in the present, the events in Vietnam in June 1963 were shocking but not life-altering. The suicides left a memorable mark, but they were more like a lightning storm that ended a baseball game but would soon burn itself out, blue skies and the resumption of our youthful insouciance soon to follow. However, for Mr. Taylor, Bobby, Mike and me, the conflict in Vietnam was not going to dissipate like a sudden summer shower. It was just building steam and was about to become deadly serious only a few years into the future, and each of our young lives would be forever changed.

A GROWING AWARENESS

The monk's act of self-immolation was quickly dismissed in America as a product of a misguided people who did not value life in the same way as we Americans. However, it was impossible to airbrush the image entirely out of our minds. The "why would anyone do that" question never relented despite repeated recoils of cognitive dissonance. "Those people just do not value life the way we do," was the most common theme. However, this first act of voluntary martyrdom would be followed by other Buddhist monks protesting the oppressive regime of South Vietnamese President Ngo Dinh Diem, an American ally/stand-in and a Roman Catholic like President Kennedy. The suicides made an impression on Kennedy, who the next day had a set of photos of the burning monk on his desk in the Oval Office.[1] By the time 1963 came to a close, Diem had been assassinated in a coup clumsily sanctioned by the Kennedy administration.[2]

Kennedy would also fall to an assassin's bullets that November but the war in that far-off country would rage on for 12 more years. The incipient tumult of the sixties was ratcheting up to launch speed, right on schedule. By the late sixties, the WW2 baby boomers were coming of age. For me, Pony League baseball and Pop-Warner football were far behind in the rear view mirror. Track and field was my new sport but even that could no longer monopolize my concentration. The war and the decision that would face me once I turned 18, or used up my student deferment, occupied more and more space on center stage. Millions of energetic, strong, passionate, young men across the country faced a present-tense challenge that would test our loyalty, conscience and sense of duty. It was a command performance none of us could avoid.

By the time I was a junior in high school, Vietnam was being widely discussed in the classroom and during extracurricular activities. St. Raphael Academy is a Christian Brothers school and it remains a thriving high school. Back then it was an all-boys school, and the proximity of the war — not the fighting itself but the effect it could possibly have on our lives — was hard to shake. By the time I was a senior in the fall of 1965, we were having spirited and wide-ranging discussions

---

[1] Kinzer, Stephen. *Overthrow*. Times Books, Henry Holt and Co. 2006,149.
[2] Ibid. 158.

about the war, especially during American history and religion classes. Our American history teacher was the tallest person in the school, our basketball team included. A veritable giant. Brother P was also a compelling teacher, supplementing our flimsy textbook with reading from a thick volume by historians Samuel Morrison and Henry Steele Commager. He was also a staunch anti-Communist. And he was not above mocking one of the more left-leaning members of the class, generally addressing him as "Comrade R."

In a display of superb showmanship, he once flipped a long knife (maybe a bayonet) into "Comrade R's" front row desk where it stuck and vibrated just a little — but a lot less than our quaking psyches. I cannot fully remember the point of his point — probably a warning to "Comrade" and any future comrades. Needless to say, though, he had our undivided attention. We were fully primed when he later produced a page of newsprint and lit it with a match. It burned slowly enough for him to equate the burning page to the dangerous spread of communism. The only way to stop its inexorable advance, he expounded while the flames inched up toward his arm, was to stomp it out. And with that, he placed the paper on a front row desk ("Comrade R's" -- I cannot be sure). With one swat of his enormous hand, Brother P snuffed it out. The smoke and smell lingered as he made his lesson crystal clear: That is the only way to put an end to the communist scourge. Stomp it out before it spreads. Wow.

On the other side of the debate was our religion and English teacher, Brother R. (I am using only an initial for privacy concerns.) His initial attempts at an exegesis of the Old Testament went nowhere, and he soon relented to a more topical approach. He moderated a free-ranging discussion covering just about everything — including the war in Vietnam, which was more his style anyway. Brother R had a master's degree In English from UC Berkeley and was perhaps the most truth-seeking teacher that I'd ever encountered. A committed Catholic, he was passionate but thoughtful. The moral question pervaded every class, but he guided our discussions — or allowed them to go — to places that would one day have him called on the carpet by his bishop. In actuality, Brother R was following the exhortations of his recently deceased pope, John XXIII, who encouraged the church to open its windows to allow in some fresh air. Questioning basic tenets of religion was fair game in Brother R's zeitgeist, much to the dismay of many parents, who had to wonder why their boys, whom they sent off in the morning to a Catholic school, were returning home in the afternoon as atheists.

The controversy sparked by Brother R's open-ended religion class was debated in a large hall filled with concerned parents, teachers and students. For St. Raphael Academy, it was an apocalyptical event. The most memorable moment came when Brother R broke through a largely unproductive back and forth and announced: "If I had my druthers, I'd much prefer a thinking atheist to a non-thinking Catholic." Talk about laying your cards on the table. Parents gasped and I have to admit I too was a bit stunned. "Did he really say that?" I thought. Sure, Brother R's comment was completely consistent with his values and *modus operandi*, but he just took a very big risk. However, if he had the courage to stand by his convictions with his job, reputation, excommunication, and perhaps his immortal soul on the line, then, by God, who was I to be any different?

Back in the mid-1960's St. Raphael was the perfect environment for a boy coming of age. There was no one-way to view reality. No group-think. We were encouraged to consider issues deeply, make moral decisions, and above all be people of conscience. Right and wrong were personal choices that required our most sincere attention. Nothing quite focuses the mind like imminent death; the prospect of dying and killing in Vietnam had definitely gotten my sincere and serious attention.

I DIDN'T GO

Well before I graduated from college and lost my student deferment, I had decided the war in Vietnam was not something I could support. It was not something I wanted to give my life for, nor was it anything that justified my taking the life of another — even if the "other" was a Vietnamese Communist. Moreover, I did not want my friends, classmates, teammates, sports rivals or fellow baby boomers to be dragged into a suspect affair that in my mind was morally unjustifiable and made no life-or-death sense. To this day I grieve over lives lost in the Vietnam War, and I have actively lobbied against recent US misadventures — the most foolish and duplicitous of them the 2003 invasion of Iraq. I wrote to my US representatives, and President Bush, begging him to hold off. Later I led a group meeting with US Representative Patrick Kennedy — a pro-Iraq invasion supporter, lobbying him to change his mind, which he eventually did. Despite my effort and desire to spare young men and women from the dictates of elected officials who all too easily commit our military to dubious campaigns, the conflicts continue and innocent foreigners as well as loyal soldiers pay the price.

However, the 2003 Iraq fiasco has surely given presidential candidates pause. Senator John Kerry and Senator Hillary Clinton voted for the 2002 Iraq Resolution. Kerry lost the general election to George W. Bush and much was made of Kerry's equivocating: "I voted against it before I voted for it." Clinton lost to Obama in the primaries and to Trump in the general. Clinton tried to distance herself from her support for the invasion but her primary opponent, Bernie Sanders — who voted "nay," never let her forget it.

As an Illinois state senator, Barack Obama was on record in his opposition to Operation Iraqi Freedom ... as was the Left's *bete noir*, Donald Trump. Each ascended to the highest office in the land, and as I write President Trump has just rejected the advice of his cabinet to punish Iran for destruction of an unmanned drone. Once Trump was told the retaliatory strike would result in 150 deaths, Trump cancelled the attack, deeming the mission simply not "proportionate" to the loss of an *unmanned* drone. For all his bluster and self-aggrandizement, Trump's decision evinced a sensibility and empathy so sadly lacking in US decision-making during the Vietnam and Iraq eras. If only Presidents Johnson and Nixon had been so deliberate, prudent and proportionate back then, and Bush-Cheney in the early 2000's. Rays of light can be reflected or refracted in myriad ways, and I, for one, am grateful the current commander-in-chief has for the moment shown appropriate and proportionate restraint. War means death — an inalterable outcome of battle. And whether it's one of "us" or "them," our political leadership needs an informed citizenry to push for an exploration of all other options. We must never ever again engage in "wars of choice," conflicts we entered even though US security was not being threatened.

Back to the Vietnam War Era: My decision to opt for peaceful resistance to the conflict in Southeast Asia was a personal one; however, I also was conscientiously objecting to war because I had higher ideals for my country, and I was hopeful that my decision would somehow bring the war to a peaceful resolution and spare young men in my age group from harm. Since then, I have still not seen a war I could support.

When under fire, soldiers become intensely loyal to each other, knowing full well that their lives are intrinsically dependent on the lives and loyal teamwork of their comrades. It is this brotherly love that keeps soldiers fighting. The death — or likely death — of a comrade is a powerful motivator. It makes soldiers hate their enemy and go hard for the kill. Despite being conceived under atrocious conditions, the love and devotion soldiers have for each other in the midst of battle is exactly what their commanders and politicians want from them. The Vietnam War soldier was in a fight for his life — and fighting for his buddies as well. He had no other option. Those of us out of harm's way had choices and I felt morally obligated to do what I could to "bring our boys home" before they were transformed into killers because of conditions beyond their control that made them that way.

Back in 1942, during the US infantry's campaign in Africa — its first theatre of combat in WW2, American soldiers were on a losing streak. However, after suffering 6000 casualties in three weeks, finally their "blood was up." Earlier in the war effort, a training manual urged commanders to "teach their men to hate the enemy — to want to kill by any means." General George S Patton told his corps, "We must be eager to kill." An officer in the 6th Infantry remarked, "A soldier is not effective until he has learned to hate. When he lives for one thing, to kill the enemy, he becomes of value." Decent human beings, American soldiers were slow to rise to this level of loathing but the deaths and injuries inflicted upon troops in Tunisia eventually changed everything. War correspondent Ernie Pyle noticed "the casual and workshop manner in which they talked about killing. They had made the psychological transition from their normal belief that taking a human life was sinful, to … where killing was a craft." Pyle added, "They lost too many friends. Soon it was killing that animated them."[3]

Vietnam came 20 years later but the peculiar dynamic that turns formerly decent men into killing machines remained the same. And I don't believe I would have been any different than the men of the 6th Infantry had I been thrust into mortal combat. The survival instinct trumps all others, and witnessing the slaughter of comrades makes a soldier's rage grow only stronger. Medicines that eradicate disease come with advisements — warnings of unpleasant and unintended consequences, side effects. If the transformation of a normal human being into a hateful, robotic killer is necessary to defeat an enemy, then the prospect of war presents us with an odious choice: hate and kill, or remain human and be killed. Neither option lifts the spirit, to say the least.

Conscientiously — I believed — and still do, perhaps even more fervently — that life is a precious gift, something entirely not our own making. Life is the sacred energy that we receive from a generous power far beyond our ability to repay, let alone control — and certainly not something to be snuffed out or sacrificed because politicians declare war upon a country that had never fired a shot in anger at the USA … until provoked.

As a matter of conscience I could not participate in a misadventure that violated everything I held sacred. The intervening years have made my decision as a 21-year-old all the more right to me now at age 70. Sometime far into the future, maybe this country will celebrate a Peace Day, during which historical opposition to war will be duly noted — not to honor or praise individuals but to lift the principle of active, non-violent resistance to war to its proper standing. War is an unacceptable alternative to conflict resolution. We need to come to terms with the irreparable damage inflicted by war upon the vanquished and victors alike.

---

[3] Atkinson, Rick. *Army at Dawn*. New York: Henry Holt and Company, 2002, 461- 2.

Living is difficult enough. Sickness, the infirmities of old age, and death — ours and those we love — are inevitable consequences of our existence. And we want to deliberately add more pain and suffering to the mix? Why? Sensible, rational, empathetic beings can do much better.

A POLITICAL PERSPECTIVE

In the autumn of 1970, I applied for conscientious objector status and received it. Agencies like the American Friends Service Committee, which counseled young men applying for conscientious objector status, listed both Pawtucket draft boards — Number 5 and Number 22 — as notoriously reluctant to grant CO's, as these deferments were called. Nevertheless, I was approved, but the full scope of the drama underlying my interview did not become known to me until nearly 50 years after the fact.

Even though I went to college in Providence just five miles from my doorstep on Walcott Street, Brown University and the Pawtucket I grew up in were a world apart. Eager and thrilled with the college scene, I was totally absorbed in my studies and with running an ever-faster quarter mile. Later, I lived for 23 years in Florida and that relocation further distanced me from my roots. Starting in about 1967, I lost touch with almost everyone from Pawtucket, and though I knew friends and acquaintances were enlisting or being drafted, I was not entirely aware of my hometown's significant presence in far off East Asia. It wasn't until I read *They Heard the Bugle's Call* that I realized how many of my peers from Pawtucket served during the Vietnam era. Unfortunately, 21 Pawtucket residents paid the ultimate sacrifice, and I am aware of at least two others whose exposure to Agent Orange led to cancer, and for at least one, death.

As I reflect on the war, and as its hidden history becomes more accessible to all, confidence in my decision to conscientiously object grows stronger and my resolve to avert a similar conflict strengthens as well. I am greatly saddened by the deaths of those I knew, and I am horrified to see similar, recent US attempts at regime change and "democratization" produce unintended, destabilizing consequences that should have been easily foreseen by high-level policy makers. The 2003 debacle in Iraq began in 2002 when President Bush referred to North Korea, Iran and Iraq as the "axis of evil" in his State of the Union address. It was a frightening metaphor and served the Bush administration's purposes quite well. The eventual invasion of a country that had done the US no wrong had as its rationale false claims that Iraq dictator Saddam Hussein had stockpiled weapons of mass destruction (WMD). That claim was based on phony evidence, however, and was as wrong as it gets. In the early stages of the war I opposed that war and disputed the WMD claim, but most of the country had been swayed. One very politically aware friend was so sure of the WMD allegations that she insisted on wagering $100 on its truthfulness. She lost her bet and to her credit promptly paid up. More germane to the flimsiness of the WMD claim, however, is that I — someone having no insider knowledge — could have been right about such a crucial fact but so many in Washington and citizens countrywide steadfastly believed in this dangerously arrogant misperception. So much so they were quite literally willing to go to war over it.

Even more preposterous were claims in 2002 and 2003 by Bush and Cheney that Saddam was going to share his WMDs with Osama bin Laden and Al Qaeda. There was no such alliance, and any thinking person should have been highly skeptical about two such obvious antagonists ever joining hands in a fiendish plot. Yet in October 2002, a Senate controlled by Democrats passed the "Iraq Resolution," 77 in favor, including every Republican, save one — R.I. Senator Lincoln Chafee. Twenty one Democrats and one Independent (Bernie Sanders) also voted nay. The domestic campaign led by the Bush-Cheney Administration was so successful at touting the need for the invasion that upwards of 73 percent of Americans favored the call to war. Putting his reputation on the line in service to the Bush-Cheney Administration, Secretary of State and retired four-star general Colin Powell gave a bravura performance at the United Nations — and in front of the entire world — testifying to the validity of the WMD accusation. Despite his sincerity and sterling reputation, Powell — a man of impeccable character — was completely wrong. A costly, bloody and ultimately destabilizing war was agitated for, launched and executed under entirely false circumstances.

Didn't anyone learn the painful lessons of Vietnam? Very few, apparently. At that time during the 1960's, the drums of war beat to the tune a different but equally compelling metaphor — the "Domino Theory," which claimed that all of Southeast Asia would fall under communist control if Vietnam, a key domino, was not rescued from the clutches of North Vietnamese leader Ho Chi Minh, a declared communist. However, the Domino Theory was a reality that never remotely came to pass. In fact, in 1978 Vietnam *overthrew* a communist regime — the Khmer Rouge in Cambodia, which was responsible for three million Cambodian deaths plus unimaginable human suffering. Then in 1979, Vietnam successfully repulsed an attack by China — the very country it was supposed to link arms with.

Vietnam was no capitulating domino. By freeing neighbor Cambodia from the fiendish Khmer Rouge and then by repelling an invasion by China, Vietnam had actually done the reverse. Vietnam's incursion into Cambodia to overthrow the murderous Khmer Rouge and then its successful, armed resistance to the Chinese invasion graphically undermined the foundation of the Domino Theory, which had been the essential reason for US military intervention. There would be no falling dominos. Over 58,000 Americans had died and more than 300,000 wounded in a valiant effort to serve a government policy that was poorly thought out and extremely flawed. Error and hubris led to the expected result — a bitter defeat made all the more memorable by America's harried exit from the country, immediately followed by the communists' triumphant takeover of Saigon.

Testifying before the Senate in 1971, then Lt. John Kerry posed the question that haunts us to this day: "How do you ask a man to be the last man to die for a mistake?" The only answers to that question is "You can't" and "You shouldn't." However, the war lasted for four more years. Instead of a litany of *mea culpas* from all those responsible for a wrongheaded decision that cost so many soldiers their lives, health and wellbeing, we got nothing. No apologies, no remorse. Unfortunately, Senator Kerry found himself on the wrong end of an irony 30 years later when he himself voted in favor of the 2002 Iraq Resolution, which was also based on a flawed premise — WMDs and an al Qaeda-Iraq conspiracy to terrorize the US.

The drumbeat to war in Vietnam was amplified by the "Second Gulf of Tonkin incident," an attack that the Pentagon Papers proved – – and then later former Secretary of Defense Robert McNamara admitted — never happened as it had been described. However, the incident served as a sufficient enough excuse for President Johnson to escalate the war effort. Then in early March 1965, Johnson initiated Operation Rolling Thunder. One afternoon during the first week of March, we heard the news. I was 16 years old, a high school junior, and running my first year of indoor track. We practiced inside the Pawtucket Armory. We were noticeably on edge all that afternoon.

In addition to the horrible loss of lives, the numerous wounded, the still rising number of PTSD cases, and the enormous cost in taxpayer dollars, our country had committed itself and (ultimately) 2.6 million brave young men to a war that made no sense, greatly diminishing our credibility internationally as well as on the home front. The Vietnamese, as it turns out were a proudly nationalistic people, willing to defend their homeland even when confronted by an American superpower or an emerging superpower like China. Ho Chi Minh had fought against Japanese invaders during WW2. The Vietnamese Constitution is patterned after our own. Ho petitioned President Truman to become a US ally. However, because he and the country had the "C word" — Communist — attached to their names, his appeal was rejected, and not too far down the line the US inherited the restive occupation that colonialist France had abandoned in 1956.

Since the turn of the millennium, four US presidents have visited Vietnam — Bill Clinton, GW Bush, Barack Obama and, most recently, Donald Trump. Vietnam currently exports numerous goods to the US, and it has siphoned off manufacturing jobs from China — once again laying bare the false claims of the Domino Theory. In hindsight, what was gained by the US? Nothing worthwhile. What was lost? American lives, American wounded, American treasure, and, perhaps most ominous for the purported leader of the free world, American credibility. Vietnam was a war of choice. As it turns out, a very bad choice fought by loyal and courageous Americans. These Vietnam Vets deserved much better.

THE PROTEST MOVEMENT

Either drafted or enlisted, numerous young men from Pawtucket found themselves in Vietnam, and 21 of them died there. At the same time, as war protests gained steam in the US during the mid-60's, a hand indignantly holding a draft card was the closest most American protesters came to a flame. Not nearly as self-sacrificing as Buddhist monks, draft-age American boys, nevertheless, repulsed and mystified many of the World War Two veterans who only a couple decades earlier had put themselves in the line of fire. Those vets made the world safe for freedom-loving people by putting the brakes on two very real evil empires — Nazi Germany and Imperial Japan.

No surprise, then, that WW2 vets felt betrayed by their very own sons, and the protests served to polarize families as well as the country. I now believe the effectiveness of the protest movement would have been greatly enhanced if we sons and daughters were not so insensitive or indifferent to the deeds of our fathers, who two decades later would be praised by these same children as "the Greatest Generation." We who opposed the war easily found agreement among ourselves, but we failed to build bridges with our fathers, uncles and neighbors, who were precisely the "silent majority" we needed to have on our side.

If there was a case to be made for a just war, WW2 was it, no doubt about it. Yes, if President Wilson had heeded to his original intent — "peace without victory," then perhaps the post-World War One turmoil generated in a defeated and economically destroyed Germany might have been avoided and the seeds of hate that produced the Nazi juggernaut might never have germinated into the Third Reich's murderous creation. But that's all hypothetical. The men and women who lived through WW2 were rightly proud of the flesh and blood loyalty they devoted to their country, which was unquestionably in the right. They came back home and started families, raising sons and daughters and opening doors to tangible opportunities that WW2 Vets could have only dreamed of. So who were these selfish kids — their kids — who could be so ungrateful and so unaware of the life and death situations their fathers faced while fighting two of the more evil empires the world has ever seen — Nazi Germany in Europe and Imperial Japan in the Pacific? If only every protest speech had begun with sincere words of gratitude to WW2 Vets, fully recognizing their sacrifices and accomplishments while at the same time pointing out pertinent and crucial differences between that war and Vietnam. The generation gap might have been bridged, the country less divided, and families more united — in particular, fathers and sons. The finding of common ground between the two wildly different generations could have created a unified voice and a powerful voting bloc. However, we Americans took a well-trod path — one that accentuated our differences rather than rallying behind a common bond.

In 1968, two assassinations — Rev. Martin Luther King, Jr. and the Democrats' leading candidate, Robert F. Kennedy — robbed the country of its two most noble and inspirational leaders. Nevertheless, the antiwar movement could not be stopped. Eugene McCarthy was a leading critic of the war and after Kennedy's assassination, now the leading spokesperson for the movement. He held a rally in Fenway Park that summer. The stadium was completely filled by the time my friend Mike and I arrived. Fire marshals had closed the stadium, barring entry to us, but we somehow evaded them and squeezed our way into one of the many overly crowded aisles. McCarthy entered from center field, standing in a convertible that dropped him off at the pitcher's mound. He spoke but did not light a fire. If it had been RFK, no doubt the assembled would have been completely inspired and sacrificed everything to work for his election. As it turned out, the Democrat's Convention in Chicago was a travesty. My friend Mike was a pre-med student and spent much time bandaging and counseling the bloodied, who got that way not because of the Viet Cong but thanks to the Chicago PD.

Former Minneapolis mayor, Minnesota Senator, Vice-President and leading liberal Hubert Humphrey was the eventual nominee. However, after the chaotic convention, the Democrats were badly splintered and the antiwar movement did not soundly support Humphrey — instead, identifying him with Johnson, the reviled escalator of the war. However if there ever was an example of the "perfect being the enemy of the good," this was it. Richard Nixon won in a close election and the war continued for another seven years. I was only 19 years old in November 1968, and too young to vote. My protest against the war would have to come as a conscientious objector, and that deadline would be upon me soon enough.

DECISION TIME 1970
...AND A GREATLY DELAYED RECKONING

Applying for a CO was pretty much constant background music throughout my college years. I became intensely focused on philosophical issues — heavy ones. My junior year I did an independent study titled: "Nihilism and Hope in the Writings of Albert Camus, Hermann Hesse and Friedrich Nietzsche." My mother once remarked, "You live too deeply." If there was any doubt about her assessment, all anyone needed to do was follow me from class to class. "The Nature of Tragedy, "Religion and Society," "Philosophy of Religion," The Complete Works of Fyodor Dostoevsky," "The Modes of Experience," "Hinduism and Buddhism," to name but a few. I had also begun working as a milieu therapist at a psychiatric hospital, which was intense as could be but it paid much better than my previous job — busboy at the Turks Head Club in downtown Providence. Through all of that intellectual turmoil, for the actual CO application I also had to get letters of reference attesting to my sincerity. I got them while at the same time writing an explanation of why I was applying for I-O status, as it was officially known. I was in it way over my head, and on so many levels. However, determined youth will generally find a way.

The last hurdle was my CO interview before the local draft board, which as I have previously mentioned, had a reputation for being none too generous about granting them. The interview was at the downtown Pawtucket post office, sometime in November of 1970, as I recall. I drove there alone. I walked into a small room and there were four older men, each wearing American flag lapels. To my great surprise, I

was acquainted with three of them. One was Mike Dalton's relative —
an older second cousin, I believe. Another was a coach from a rival
baseball team and the third was Mr. Taylor, my own Pony League
coach. They seemed a bit shocked, perhaps even a little betrayed, that
one of their own would not want to fight for his country. They began
by asking me if I'd agree to be drafted if the Russians landed on Cape
Cod. I said I would not. Thankfully, they did not ask me if I would
have fought during WW2 because that would have taken some explain-
ing and perhaps even some dissembling, which would have ruined the
spirit of things for sure. Then I was asked if I'd fight back if someone
attacked my mother. And I said I would. "Then you would use violence?" they asked by way of emphasis or clarification, I wasn't sure
which. I said that I didn't think defending my mother was an act of
violence but more an act of self-defense. "But you would fight for your
mother?" they persisted. "With everything I have," I answered, feeling
quite doomed. Honest but doomed. They got me ... But I was wrong.
They said in near unison, "Well, we think that's great because we get
guys in here all the time whining about how they can't stand the sight
of blood and ..."

A few weeks later the papers arrived in the mail. I had been
granted a CO. I was certainly relieved but wasn't about to celebrate
because I believed I hadn't really done anything. An unjust, senseless
and immoral war continued to proceed full bore, and thousands of
Americans as well as hundreds of thousands Vietnamese were dying
because of it. I wasn't about to celebrate until there was a peaceful
resolution, which, sadly, never happened

I was indeed drafted but because of my I-O status I did alternative service for two years at Butler Hospital. Life was good. However, it wasn't until nearly 50 years later that I became aware of a drama
far more intense and personal than my own that must have been playing
out during my CO interview in late 1970. You see, Mr. Taylor's son
and our intrepid shortstop/cornerback Bobby Taylor had been killed in
action in February 1969. As a soldier, Bobby was as fearless as ever.

"He took a liking to walking 'point' — first man out on patrols,
cutting through the jungle, exposing himself to enemy fire and explosive devices buried in the ground ... On February 27, 1970, Bobby

stepped on a land mine and died aboard a helicopter on his way to hospital. True to form, Booby's main concern was not for himself but for his Vietnamese scout. "How's my scout?" he asked before passing out.[4]

For the past two years I've wondered what was Mr. Taylor thinking and feeling. Bobby was a stalwart infantry man. He had made the ultimate sacrifice just a year or so earlier, yet here I was petitioning to be removed from the conflict altogether. I would never have to dodge a bullet, avoid a mine, sweat my butt off in an equatorial jungle, or endure paralyzing fear. If granted a CO, like a pampered pitcher, I was asking to be excused from the rough and tumble of front lines. I wasn't going to get my uniform dirty ... I wasn't going to even get a uniform. I'd be staying stateside doing alternative service even though Bobby was crawling through the thickets, hunting for mines before he eventually stepped on one. Had Mr. Taylor seen enough death, or had the entire group of four already seen enough carnage suffered by Pawtucket boys. I'll never know, but one thing I'm certain of: It took a mighty big person to grant a CO to me even though his own son had risked it all for his country, never to enjoy the peace and freedom of his homeland ever again.

MIKE DALTON

I cannot remember the last time I spoke with Mike Dalton. It was, for sure, during the summer, and definitely the late sixties. I clearly remember the moment though not every detail of our conversation. We were standing in front of my house. Mike looked trim and fit; I had long, scraggly hair and wore striped bell bottoms. He told me he was about to enter officer candidate school and asked me about my plans. I told him I thought the war was wrong and I was going to apply for a CO. What happened after that, I don't recall. Probably not much of anything. Because what's there to say when one person is going to offer his life in service to his country and the other person is saying his country is making a mistake? And that's the way it was. Two kids who

---

[4] Nau, Terry L. *They Heard the Bugle's Call.* Terry Nau. 2016.

had been so connected parted ways and there was much else but an awkward silence.

When I learned of Mike's death in June of 1971, I was never more devastated. I cried plenty as a little kid but as a teenager and young adult, never. Now at age 22, I could not stop crying. I cried when I told my girlfriend later that day. I cried when I locked eyes with Mike's family. Years later, I cried when I approached the Wall in DC and could not gather myself enough to look for Mike's name. And I'm crying now as I recall his passing, crying a whole lot in fact. If you live long enough, you're going to take your lumps. I've had my share, but in general I've been very blessed. However, this loss is particularly painful because, because ... I can't really find the reason.

I suppose, though, when you've first looked upon a world full of magic and possibility and you found a friend who was as innocent as you ... but not quite as naive because he was a little older and he knew some of the snares and pitfalls and he was looking out for you so you didn't get hurt and sometimes encouraging you, lifting you up so you could succeed, then it's quite a loss when all of a sudden he's gone. Gone and I never got to say "thank you"; gone and I never could tell him how much he meant to me; gone and I never got the chance to say goodbye. And gone because of a war of choice that he so patriotically and courageously entered because that's just the way Mike was.

FINAL THOUGHTS

In the intervening years, my opposition to war has been mirrored by an unlikely group — the US military. In 1991 during the lead up to the first Gulf War, the upper echelon — including Chief of Staff General Colin Powell — advocated for the use of such superior force costing only a minimum of US casualties. They also insisted on clearly defined objectives — how will we know when we've been victorious and will we know when to apply the brakes. Once Iraq had retreated from Kuwait, the goal of the mission had been accomplished and President George H.W. Bush did not order the military to pursue the conquest into Baghdad. Ironically, Powell let himself be used to foment a chimerical war plan in 2003, which just goes to show how eternally vigilant an opponent to war must be. As conflict with Iran approaches in the summer of 2019, cabinet hawks are pushing for a military response whereas military advisors to President Trump are urging restraint. The professional military knows full well the costs they and those under their command will bear.

Because who really pays the price of a bad decision? It's the American soldier and his family, plus the enemy combatants and citizens of a foreign land who have even less to say than an American citizen.

And why should the American soldier be the one to bear the pain? Young men and women who willingly put their lives on the line for country are exactly the kind of quality individuals the country should be honoring even before they've fired a weapon in anger. Instead, politicians ensconced in the safety of their secure positions and safe neighborhoods have committed these admirable heroes to many deadly endeavors, which in the end have proved to be foolishly conceived and/or poorly planned. Yet carry them out, these soldiers do.

Consider what Mike Dalton wrote to President Nixon in May 1971, while Mike was sitting in "the steaming jungle" and less than a month before his life was ended by an enemy mine. Mike was writing words of encouragement to President Nixon because "As an infantry platoon leader, I think I can begin to appreciate the pressures, pains, and satisfactions of someone in the position of decision maker ..." Mike goes on to tell the President that even within his own platoon there are soldiers both pro and con regarding the merits of the war.

Mike offers his support for the war and encourages President Nixon, but not before he writes, "Naturally, I do not enjoy being here, nor do I enjoy in any way, the thought of war. However ... I do understand and feel a moral obligation as an American, to help defend this country against communism."[5]

Such honesty, morality, loyalty and dedication to duty that the planet should simply stop spinning for a moment and shower him and others like him with our sincerest respect.

---

[5] Stephen, Donald E. *Bait. St. Joseph, Illinois:* L&L Printing, Introduction.

In Plato's *Republic*, Socrates defines the ideal "guardian of the state" as a person who over the "whole course of their lives is found to be full of zeal to do whatever they believe is for the good of the commonwealth and never against its interest."

Socrates' ideal was based on a hypothetical, but Mike Dalton, and Bobby Taylor as well, were the real deal. They, and too many others like them, paid the ultimate price, unfortunately, a price that was ultimately unnecessary and costly beyond measure.

As citizens, it is our moral calling to do everything legally possible to urge our government to find a saner way to resolve our conflicts, assuage our fears, and build a lasting peace. Even if the most we can do is say "No." Individuals and nations will forever have their differences, but it is upon us the breathing and thinking to do whatever necessary to prevent such heartrending, irrevocable, losses from ever happening again.

A CUT ABOVE THE REST – Michael Dalton was held in the highest esteem by everyone who knew him. A star athlete in high school, Michael became an infantry officer in Vietnam and died ten weeks after his son Scott was born in April 1971. (Photo courtesy of the Dalton family)

FAMILY TRADITION – *Vietnam veteran Michael Yatsko, right, poses with his son Joseph and grandson Nicholas. All three were military veterans who went on to become police officers. Mike's brother Joe died in the Vietnam War. (Photo courtesy of the Yatsko family.)*

CHAPTER TEN
Families Feel True Pain of War

BY TERRY NAU

The term "Greatest Generation" as applied to our World War II heroes did not come into vogue until the mid-1980s after popular NBC news anchor Tom Brokaw attended the 40th anniversary ceremony of the D-Day invasion. Brokaw designated the phrase for those people who grew up during the Great Depression and then labored to help win World War II, either as soldiers, essential workers or brothers and sisters laboring at home as the losses mounted overseas. The down side of this greatness is sons coming home in coffins, their memories relegated to family scrapbooks upon receipt of a cold telegram from the government. The Greatest Generation's survivors overcame these losses and then provided a foundation of prosperity for their own children, who grew up in a much better world than they did.

While the Vietnam War in no way compares to World War II, our generation of Baby Boomers is proud to be known as sons and daughters of the Greatest Generation. Sure, we were the first generation to actually question our country's motives for fighting communism 10,000 miles from home, but most of us answered the call when it came time to serve. The "Domino Theory" may seem misguided in retrospect but some serious people believed in it throughout the 1950s and 1960s, legendary men like Dwight Eisenhower and John F. Kennedy ... you know, the best and brightest of the Greatest Generation. The people who fought in World War II. There was no reason to doubt what they told us in speeches we heard on television or read in the newspapers.

Vietnam came along two decades after WW II, in an era when television and free speech were really beginning to flex their muscles. The Baby Boomers were conflicted by this simmering new "conflict" playing out halfway around the world in the rice paddies, villages and thick jungles of Vietnam. We saw bits and pieces of the action on television in the early 1960s, including three weeks before JFK's assassination when the leader of South Vietnam was brutally murdered in a military coup thought to be approved by JFK. None of that historical insight was reported at the time. A new leader took over in South Vietnam. When JFK's successor, Lyndon Baines Johnson, won a landslide election victory in November 1964, the big Texan's attention soon turned to winning that little war over in Southeast Asia. Instead of sending American "advisers" to help the South Vietnamese fight their war, LBJ sent in the Ninth Marine Division in early 1965. All hell would break loose over the next three years. America went from having 19,000 advisers in Vietnam in 1964 to over 500,000 soldiers encamped there by 1968.

So that's where the sons of the Greatest Generation came into play. We were raised by parents whose lives were seriously impacted by World War II. We were influenced by all the television shows popular in the 1950s and early 1960s, including "Combat" and "The Gallant Men" that drew on WW II for subject matter. We outgrew the Cowboys and Indians shows of the 1950s but war still had an aura that was hard to ignore. The biggest war of them all had ended less than 20 years earlier. We saw slices of it on television in historical shows like "*Victory at Sea*," or in war movies like "*The Longest Day*" that put Hollywood's spin on the D-Day Invasion.

When the oldest sons of the Baby Boomers came of fighting age in the 1960s, they just assumed some kind of military experience might be in their future. In the blue-collar town of my youth, a new community northeast of Philadelphia called Fairless Hills, very few of us thought otherwise. You could see the impact up and down our street as the eldest sons graduated from high school and signed up for the Army or the Navy, maybe even the Air Force or Marines. What choice did they have? It was either college, the military or the steel mill. Those were all good choices in a country whose future seemed so bright. Little did we know that the steel industry would fade away over the next two decades, and America's bright promise as the new leader of the Free World would come under attack because of its involvement in Vietnam.

On Cardiff Road in Fairless Hills, Larry Marsden left the house next to us in 1962 and joined the Army. His unit deployed to the Dominican Republic in 1964 to quell a rebellion. Jerry Ross from down the street joined the Army and became an early visitor to Vietnam. He would serve three tours in that war zone. Three of his brothers – Cliff, Bob and Gene -- would follow Jerry into the military. Bob would serve a year in Vietnam, too.

In my family, brother Tim joined the Air Force in 1963, stunning his parents, who had planned for each of their four sons to graduate from college. Tim pointed out that the G.I. Bill would pay for his college after he served four years in the Air Force. And he was right. It paid for mine, too, after a year in Vietnam. Older brother Dan took a circuitous route into the Army, graduating from college at the age of 25 and then joining up when the draft board came chasing after him in 1967.

Over in nearby Levittown, David Christian's older brother Doug joined the Army and went off to Vietnam before most of us could even locate the country on a world globe. David would follow in his footsteps. Younger brother Daniel, seven years younger than David, also joined the Army but was injured in training and did not get to Vietnam.

Another Levittowner, Joe Yatsko, a well-known athlete in the late 1950s at Pennsbury High School, quit college and joined the Army in 1962. He would become an officer, an airborne infantry soldier, and the first casualty from Lower Bucks County when he walked into an ambush on Dec. 18, 1965. Joe's body was escorted home by his brother Mike, who was stationed five miles away, not far from Saigon. Joe's widow Mary later joined the Army as a nurse and retired as a Lt. Colonel after more than 20 years in uniform.

Lt. Yatsko's death was a great wakeup call for Lower Bucks County. And while it sent chills up our spines, a lot of my contemporaries continued to sign up for the military and the exciting possibility of going to war. They were 19 and full of fight. Some of us were less eager to go but went nonetheless. We all came home a bit confused by what we had seen. And always proud to have served, even if our government and military leaders danced a fine line between trying to win the war and keeping the Russians and Chinese from intervening, as they had done in Korea just 20 years earlier.

It took a long time for me to figure out the true cost of war, the impact of those 58,318 deaths on families and communities across America. At first, I could see the price in the sad eyes and demeanor of two sets of parents from my neighborhood whose sons were killed in 1968. But for the longest time, I looked away, until nearly 50 years had passed and I decided to write a book about the 15 KIAs from my high school. My research soon took me to the home of Mike Yatsko, who told me the raw details of his journey home with his brother's coffin, and the big cargo plane that was filled with coffins, row upon row, from front to back of the plane. Mike wanted to find Joe's coffin but the pilot asked him to come sit up front with him for the long flight across the Pacific Ocean.

Later on, I visited with Helen Yatsko, in the Levittown home where she raised her three sons – Joe, Mike and John (who also joined the Army). Helen was in her late 80s by then. Still reluctant to speak about Joe after all these years, she simply escorted me to a row of photos on the wall of her living room, all military photos of the various Yatskos who had served their country, dating from World War II on through the Persian Gulf War of the early 1990s and into Afghanistan in 2011 where her great-grandson Nicholas had served. (Helen's grandson, Michael Yatsko Jr., served in the Gulf War.)

Mike Yatsko got married after he returned to civilian life with a bad case of PTSD. He became the father of two boys, Joseph and Michael Jr. They would both join the Army after graduating from high school. Joseph, named after his uncle, eventually became the keeper of the flame for all the family military memorabilia, excluding those photos on his grandmother's living room wall.

"As a kid, you walked into that house and you just knew that the military tradition was sacred," Joe Yatsko said to me over the phone in March 2019. "Mike and I were not really pushed into the Army. But we always knew there was a great sense of pride in what Uncle Joe and my father had done. That wall in my grandmother's house told you that. My father never really discussed his service until we got older. I know there was always a great respect for the flag in our house. My father was a great role model for me and my brother. We both followed his footsteps into the Army."

ONLY CHRISTMAS TOGETHER – Mary and Joe Yatsko spent the Christmas of 1964 together as newlyweds. 1st Lt. Yatsko died on Dec. 18, 1965 during a Viet Cong ambush just north of Saigon. (Photo courtesy of the Yatsko family)

Joseph Yatsko went on active duty after graduating from Pennsbury in 1987.

"I committed to the Army in 1986 on a delayed entry program," he said. "The delayed entry program offered the chance to get training as a military policeman. My dad had been a policeman for 30 years and he told me this was a chance to get my training in. At 18, you are too young to become a policeman in civilian life. But the Army gave me the training and when I got out three years later, I was accepted into a Police Academy out near Harrisburg and took a job in York County in 1990 as a policeman. I tell kids now that they can get a lot out of the military if they do it the right way, and get training in a field that interests them."

Mike Yatsko Jr. graduated from Pennsbury in 1991 and went straight into the Army, participating in the Gulf War.

"Mike went off to basic that summer. He became a cavalry scout," Joe Yatsko said. "They went in with the spearhead of troops in Desert Storm. If you remember, the war started with several days of bombing from the air. The troops in the spearhead had to clean up what the air war had pretty much demolished. I think that was hard on those soldiers who went in first. They saw a lot of death and destruction. Mike struggled to hold a steady job when he came home. But he took care of our grandmother after he got settled. Mike died of cancer in December 2018 at the age of 46. I don't know if the cancer could be traced to the war but I do know the war impacted him mentally."

Joe's son Nicholas graduated from high school in 2011 and went straight into the Army, and over to Afghanistan. Like his father and grandfather before him, Nicholas became a policeman after leaving the Army.

Joe points out that his family's military tradition dates back to his mother's father, Raymond Rendelman.

"He served with General Patton's Third Armored Division in Africa and then in France," Joe said.

Looking back over his family's military history, Joe Yatsko revealed a thoughtful side.

"There was a time when I would have said that everybody should serve," he admitted. "But as you get older and wiser, you realize the military is not for everybody. I definitely feel like it was our family's calling to serve. I know with my grandmother losing her oldest son in Vietnam, and my father experiencing what he did in that war, despite all the loss and the hardships, our family tradition is always spoken of in a very proud manner. I have seen some families who resent what the service did to them, but for us it is a very revered time in our lives."

***

David Christian's immediate family military history traces back to his parents.

"My mother, Dorothy, grew up in Croydon, not far from Philadelphia," said Christian, who would become one of the nation's most decorated soldiers of the Vietnam War. "She joined the Women's

Army Corps (WAC) and served on General MacArthur's staff, typing up press releases. She was with the General in the Philippines, and returned with him to the islands. My father was a 'courageous' typewriter repairman in the Army. That's how he met my mother. Dad was very tall, around 6-foot-4, and my mom was 4-foot-11 but they hit it off. Mom was very proud of her service, even though when she came home, women were not allowed into VFW posts. They were not open to women until the 1980s."

DOROTHY CHRISTIAN NAU
On Gen. MacArthur's staff

Doug Christian, two years older than David, joined the Army and went to Vietnam in 1965.

"Doug was assigned to work in chemical warfare," Dave said. "He spent four years in Vietnam. Why? Doug had a pretty good life over there. He was an E4 already and had his own hooch (living quarters). He fell in love with a Vietnamese girl. I remember him telling me that he was going to marry a Vietnamese woman and asked me what I thought. I was all for it. But there was so much bureaucracy to go through to bring a Vietnamese civilian out of the country. The Army was against soldiers marrying Vietnamese citizens. That broke Doug's heart. He was like a lost puppy when he came home. Because of a serious knee injury he suffered in Vietnam, Doug should have been on full disability. The Army gave him 10 percent and discharged Doug.

"Side effects from Agent Orange is what killed him. Doug was pretty tall, around 6-foot-1, and for the last 10 years of his life he weighed around 90 pounds because of all the cancer. He had growths all over his skin after he came home from the war. He developed gangrene in his bad leg, which had titanium implants running up and down as the result of the injury he suffered in Vietnam. I went to the doctor's office with him and saw how they would cut the growths off and put them into Gerber's baby bottles. These bottles would be injected with chemicals for testing purposes. I told Doug this had to be illegal. Those growths turned into cancer later in his life. I buried Doug in Washington Crossing National Cemetery."

David served in the war zone from June 1, 1968 until Feb. 24, 1969. He arrived at age 19, already a Lieutenant, leading small recon platoons into combat, winning the Distinguished Service Cross for extraordinary heroism, two Silver Stars, two Bronze Stars for valor, seven Purple Hearts, and a Legion of Merit, along with other medals too numerous to mention. He was burned over more than a third of his body as the result of a friendly fire napalm incident that ended his service in the war. He left the Army with the rank of Captain in 1970, having spent many long months at Valley Forge Military Hospital.

Having a soldier in the war impacted the entire family, from parents, to siblings and wives. David's wife, Peggy, visited her husband in a Tokyo hospital during December 1968 after one of his wounds sent him to the sidelines. She was seven months pregnant with the couple's first child, Colleen.

"I was doing okay in December when Peggy saw me," Christian remembered. "My right hand was paralyzed by a tiny piece of shrapnel that was so small, the doctors couldn't find it. But the CIA wanted to deploy me back to the war zone. They told me not to tell Peggy. I asked them how could I fight with a paralyzed right hand and they said not to worry, they just wanted me for my brain and my experience in combat. A month later, I was hit by napalm in a friendly fire incident and went back to Japan. Peggy had received telegrams before from the Army. But this one said 'death is imminent.' She couldn't believe it because she had just seen me a month before. Peggy did not know I had been sent back to Vietnam. To this day, she doesn't like to talk about the war. She keeps all the telegrams she got in a safe deposit box at the bank."

Younger brother Daniel Christian turned 17 in 1972. His future was almost predestined.

"Daniel is seven years younger than me," David Christian said. "Our whole family was Army. Every year we would watch the Bing Crosby movie, *White Christmas*, which was about a General coming back to his troops at Christmas. That was a very moving story for us. Daniel was much closer to our stepfather, Tony Nau, a World War II veteran. Our mom, who died in 1968, and our father were both WW II veterans. The whole neighborhood in Levittown was filled with WW II veterans. Daniel signed up as soon as he could. It was just a natural thing to do. He hurt his knee in training at Fort Polk when his leg got caught in the track of an armored vehicle. Daniel joined the Army to be an engineer, however his military service was interrupted after his injury. Today, Daniel is a disabled veteran who works as an electrician. Daniel is doing well. He comes to our Veterans Wellness Programs at the Levittown/Fairless Hills YMCA with his wife.

"My sister Dorothea married a Navy guy named Stanley Swain who returned from Vietnam with problems for life," Christian said. "You could say our family was very committed to serving the country."

***

While researching my books on Vietnam War casualties from Lower Bucks County and Pawtucket, I gained a real appreciation of the pain that Gold Star families still feel over the loss of their brothers or their husbands a half-century ago. The sister of Michael McGinnis broke a gear shift off in her car, not out of anger, but from the tension that built up when the terrible news came to her parents' home. The widow of Michael Dalton told me she still dreams of her first husband, her true love. Cathy Maciminio spoke of those days following the death of her husband, Tony, in 1966, when her world was falling apart. How do you put the pieces back together? These women were all young and they recovered in time to raise families and live full lives, but that hole in their heart never completely healed.

***

And then there are the Agent Orange casualties, the aging veterans who came down with soft-tissue cancer, leukemia, Hodgkin's Disease and a variety of other diseases that have been linked to the deadly dioxin.

Agent Orange became personal to me the day before my high school class's 50th reunion in 2015. I was talking to a classmate, Ed McGurk, who had been afflicted with a cancer traced to Agent Orange. The Veterans Administration had approved his disability compensation.

"They're paying me to die," Ed said with a rueful smile. At that point in time, he had less than five years to live.

In high school, Eddie was always smiling. He had been the most popular kid in our class of 725 students, a big guy who played football and wrestled at heavyweight. He served on the Student Council. Ed enrolled at Ball State University in Indiana where he played on the football team before the draft got him. The always jovial young man worked on the OV1-Mohawk.

Ed came home and never missed a beat. He worked his way up in the automobile market as a salesman and manager. He became the father of three beautiful children. At one point, Ed co-owned a dealership in Jenkintown, just outside of Philadelphia. Life was good. But then the cancer hit him in his 60s, four decades after he returned from Vietnam.

In the winter of 2018-19, Ed's condition turned for the worse. He died on May 29, 2019, a shell of his old self. Agent Orange had claimed another victim from Pennsbury High.

Other victims of Agent Orange from Pennsbury included Floyd Dellagnena, Ben Churchill, Terry Bender, Lee Miles and Jake Rees, to name the ones we know about. There are certainly more. Many of them went off to war willingly, taking that deal the government was making in those days. If you get killed in the war, your next of kin cashes in a $10,000 life insurance policy the government took out when you went to Vietnam. What the soldiers did not know was the government was spraying Agent Orange all over the countryside in Vietnam, trying to eliminate vegetation that would serve as hiding places for the enemy.

Floyd Dellagnena's widow, Martha, remembered her husband talking about his duty as a special ops soldier, on a mission across the border in Laos. The soldiers in his unit looked up in the sky to see American planes flying low, spreading a mist over the treetops, right above their heads. They asked their commanding officer what this was. He asked his superiors back at headquarters. They asked someone else higher on the military's chain of command. The word came back: Don't worry about it.

"They said they were just trying to cut down the jungle growth," Martha Dellagnena recalled in 2014. "I guess they weren't telling the truth at the time."

Floyd died in 2008 after his body began taking on fluids, forcing his weight over 300 pounds. Because Floyd's unit served in a top secret operation across the Vietnam/Laos border, there were no official records of their actions. When Floyd applied for disability compensation after his cancer first appeared in 2002, the VA denied his claims at first.

"Floyd had been retaining a lot of fluid," Martha Dellagnena told the author for the book, *'We Walked Right Into It: Pennsbury High and the Vietnam War.'* He eventually got up to 350 pounds from all that fluid inside his body. The doctors thought it might be asbestos poisoning. After they looked him over for a while, they decided his problems were connected to Agent Orange. He finally got some disability money after we went through yards and yards of paperwork. Floyd started reading a lot of books about Agent Orange. He was trying to find out how it affected other soldiers who served in the war. Floyd just got sicker and sicker. He died on Nov. 21, 2008 at the age of 61. It was a terrible way to die."

BACK HOME – Tim Stives and his wife, Christine, leave Eisenhower Chapel at Penn State following their wedding on June 14, 1969. (Photo courtesy of Christine Stives)

CHAPTER ELEVEN
The Wives Waited At Home

BY TERRY NAU

You don't hear too much about the women behind the soldiers who go to war. The vast majority of soldiers in the Vietnam War were 19 or 20 years old and hadn't settled down yet when their draft notice came, or when they enlisted. But there were soldiers who made it through college before Vietnam took them away from home. They had time to get married. Some were enrolled in ROTC in college and knew they had an active duty commitment to fulfill as soon as they graduated. Wives would wait for them longer than a girlfriend.

Christine Stives and Arlene Carter are two wives I spoke to for this chapter. They were the lucky ones, and they know it. Their husbands made it home safely, making life an even more precious affair for both of these women and their husbands, Tim Stives and Mike Carter.

"Tim was commissioned a 2nd Lieutenant and graduated on the same day, June 14, 1969," Christine Stives said, remembering that date so well because only a week earlier, she and Tim were married in a military ceremony, complete with saber bearers, in the chapel at Penn State.

Christine had grown up in western Pa., north of Pittsburgh, while Tim came from eastern Pa., perhaps 350 miles away. They met at Penn State and clicked, despite knowing that the Vietnam War would probably figure in their future within a year or two. Tim had committed to ROTC on a college campus that did not begin protesting the war in earnest until 1970.

Arlene Carter first met her husband in high school in Pawtucket, R.I.

"We were 16 years old," Arlene said in the spring of 2019. "I was a student at Tolman and Mike was over at St. Raphael Academy. We were leading what I thought were typical lives. We had loving parents, we went to school and to proms. We aspired to go to college. After high school, I went to Rhode Island College and Mike to Providence College where he joined the ROTC. When you are that young, life is just the next thing you do. Mike wanted to serve in the military and I was going to support him in whatever way I could."

Mike and Arlene were married in 1968. Arlene was pregnant while Mike attended officer's basic training at Fort Lee in Virginia. The baby went full term but was born with an inoperable lung disease and died two days after birth. Arlene almost lost her own life during the delivery.

"When we lost the baby, the doctors said it was just one of those things. No reason why we can't have another. Right away, we started trying. Mike was going to Jump School at the time and then he would have to attend Rigger School. We knew that there were only two Lieutenant slots for riggers in Vietnam so we figured he would not be going there right away. The day after I found out I was pregnant, Mike received his orders for Vietnam. That was really tough, especially after losing a child, and knowing I would have to face this alone. But the support of my family and friends helped me through. I moved back in with my parents. That was the practical thing to do. During my first pregnancy, I had lost a tremendous amount of blood. I was on special medications to make sure I would survive my second pregnancy."

After training they headed to Mike's first Army assignment with the 82nd Airborne at Fort Bragg, located in Fayetteville, N.C.

"I found that life in the South was very difficult," Arlene said firmly. "My background was in social work. During that period in the 1960s, I admired John F. Kennedy, Robert Kennedy and Martin Luther King. When we went down south, it was a real awakening for me for a few reasons. To see that segregation still existed was very surprising to me, a girl raised in New England. I will never forget when we drove over the state line into North Carolina, we saw a big billboard that showed someone in a white hooded uniform, waving a torch. Underneath, it said, 'Welcome to North Carolina, home of the Ku Klux Klan.'

The sign must have been on private property. That was shocking to me. Although the Civil Rights Act of 1964 prohibited segregation, the physical evidence of segregation still existed. This was very surprising to me, a girl raised in New England. I was so naïve. We kept seeing two of everything – two elementary schools, one on each side of the street. It took me a minute to figure out one was previously for white children and the other for black children. Two sets of bathrooms, one previously for whites only, the other for blacks. We had never seen this before back home."

Christine Stives had her own first impressions to deal with.

"The day after Tim was commissioned and graduated, we packed all our stuff in our 1966 Ford Mustang and drove straight to Fort Benning, Ga. for Infantry Officer's Basic Course and the para-troopers' school. I sort of liked Army life. We had both grown up in modest circumstances and this was the first time we had any spending money. Everything was very inexpensive on the post. You could order a hamburger and fries for one dollar and a drink for 50 cents. Our living quarters were nice enough, and very easy on our budget. My only com-plaint was the weather. It was hot as hell in Georgia!"

Stives' first assignment took him to Germany. The world was opening up to this young soldier and his wife.

"We were stationed at Wildflecken, a NATO training com-pound with U.S. and West German troops. It was only two kilometers from the border with East Germany, near the Fulda Gap, which was considered to be a place where the Russians were most likely to invade West Germany. It was 1970, just 25 years after the end of WWII, and the Cold War was still very hot. To slow down any advancing Russian troops, no autobahns or major highways extended up to this region. It was a very poor, backward agricultural area. Many people didn't have hot running water in their homes and they used outhouses. But we lived in a very nice duplex home on the base that during the war had housed Hitler's SS troops. Tim had taken German in high school and a lot of it came back to him when he was around German speakers so whenever we left the base, he had a great time talking with the locals. They ap-preciated an American who could speak their language. We had a good year there. Munich was only four hours away. Paris was six hours away, so we tried to travel as much as possible. Since we really didn't have a honeymoon, Tim got leave and we went to Brussels, Paris and Normandy for our first anniversary."

Mike Carter went to war in the spring of 1969. He was stationed at Cam Ranh Bay, a big post and air base located along the eastern coast of Vietnam. It was relatively safe, except for the random mortar and rocket attacks. (His final month would become precarious as Mike was assigned to provide support for the Cambodian Incursion in the spring of 1970.)

"We communicated mostly by letters," Arlene said. "There was a phone in Mike's office. He had a ham radio station in his unit. They would contact ham operators in the states who would then patch telephone calls to relatives. Whenever they had an open line, Mike would put in a call to me. It was primarily a one-way radio connection so 'I love you ... over' became a joke with us. I got most of my news about the war from television. It was good to know Mike was in a fairly safe place. I had joined a Wives Club and listened to some of the infantry wives talk about their husbands and where they were fighting. I felt thankful. I didn't know when he went into Cambodia because he didn't want me to worry."

Tim Stives reached Vietnam relatively late in the war, arriving in February 1971, when fighting had become more complicated because the U.S. was already beginning to withdraw troops from Vietnam.

"Tim got his orders at the end of 1970," Chris Stives said. "I didn't want to go live with my parents. By that time, I was living independently of them. I didn't think it would be a good idea to go back. We rented an apartment in Fairless Hills, down by the old 'Big C' store. I got a job because I had to do something. I could not sit home all day and wait for the news to come on television."

By now a 1st Lt., Tim Stives would lead infantry patrols into the jungle, sometimes for a week or more.

"We communicated entirely by letter," Chris Stives admitted. "Tim couldn't carry a tape recorder in his backpack. He could barely carry what he really needed. I would get a letter every five or six days. Sometimes two or three would come at the same time because Tim was often in the jungle where there were no places to mail. I understood it was hard for him to write to me."

Knowing her husband was living like a survivalist, Christine Stives began sending "Care" packages to Tim, a common practice among families with soldiers in a war zone.

"Tim was eating MREs (meals ready to eat) out of little green cans," she said. "They were greasy. And the water was bad. Within two or three weeks, Tim's digestive system was shot. I started sending Tim little baggies of instant rice with salt and pepper added. Seal them in a baggy. He could heat them up himself. That was the only food his stomach could tolerate. Fortunately, Tim could eat some 'normal' food when they went back to the base in between missions."

Arlene Carter lived carefully back home in Pawtucket as her pregnancy advanced. She found herself reacting to the protestors that were on television news almost every night.

"I had a problem with the protestors," she admitted. "It's hard to explain. I just felt like they did not really understand what was going on with our soldiers. They did not know why Mike was there. It was a matter of patriotism to us, following what your President asked you to do. Vietnam was something we supported, because our country was backing the Vietnamese people. When Mike got back home, everyone else his age had moved on with their careers, their jobs. Mike had his uniform on when he arrived at Green Airport. He met his son Michael for the first time at the airport. And that was the only time Mike wore his uniform. He never wore it again. He still had a few years obligation in the inactive reserves, but Mike was never called back to duty. It was just difficult because of the way our country was at the time. I have to say, most of our friends were very supportive. We did not have any anti-war people in our crowd.

"We had to start all over again when Mike came home," Arlene Carter added. "There were not many jobs available. It was a hard thing to get through that stage in our lives."

What did that one year teach Arlene Carter?

"I learned about the unpredictability of life," she said. "Mike lost some friends in Vietnam – Tom Gill, Mike Dalton and Jack Hulme. He always had a deep sense of patriotism. And after he retired, Mike did not want to sit back and just relax. He wanted to give something back. Mike got involved with the local Veterans of Foreign Wars and began helping out with community events and veterans ceremonies. This is something he wanted to do."

SEPARATED BY WAR – Mike and Arlene Carter are shown during their R&R vacation in Hawaii, a welcome hiatus from the Vietnam War. (Photo courtesy of Arlene Carter)

Mike Carter was named Commander of the Rhode Island VFW on June 1, 2019. But what really matters to Mike and Arlene is their two sons, Michael and Christopher.

"We also have two wonderful daughters-in-law and three beautiful grandchildren," Arlene said, proudly.

Mike Carter got home in 1970, a year before Tim Stives went to war. Christine Stives would mark the days off her calendar during that long 1971 campaign. She worked, shopped, visited Tim's grandparents, and watched the news on television every night.

"The scariest moment of my 12 months came one day when I was coming back from shopping," Christine recalled. "I had taken the first set of bags from the car and up to my apartment. I went back to the car and grabbed the rest. As I arrived at my doorstep, I saw an Army staff car pull into the parking lot. A soldier in uniform and another man got out. They started walking towards my building. I dropped the bags and started to cry because I was sure they were there to inform me of Tim's death. But they walked right past my door."

Tim Stives actually came home twice from Vietnam.

"Let me explain," Chris Stives said. "Every soldier got R&R leave from Vietnam. As the war wound down, the Army gave officers the option of flying home at their own expense for R&R. They could take two weeks leave. Well, it just so happened my parents' 25th wedding anniversary happened in September. We put up $1,000 to fly Tim home as a surprise to them. One thousand dollars was a lot of money at the time! The hardest thing I ever did was put Tim back on the plane for Vietnam a second time. You could still go to the gate at airports in those days. I sat with Tim at the gate. I held it together and as soon as he was out of sight, I ran into the lady's room and just lost it."

The second time, Tim tried to surprise his wife. He had received his orders to come home one month earlier than anticipated. So he didn't tell anyone. Just flew into San Francisco and called Christine at 2 in the morning.

"I had been told that soldiers could only call home if they were wounded," Christine said. "That way, the family member on the other end would know right away that he was okay. So when Tim called at 2 in the morning, I was in a deep haze. When he said, 'This is Tim. I am in San Francisco,' all I could think of was to ask, 'How badly are you hurt?' We did that a couple times before Tim got it through to me that he was okay and he was coming home. I remember him asking me to

151

bring a jacket with me to the airport because the Army had sent these soldiers home in January in their tropical uniforms with no jackets."

Stives, now a Captain, had two more years left on his commitment, but the hard part was over. His next duty station was to Fort Lewis, Washington, where he served with the 9th Infantry Division in various positions.

"One day, Tim's boss said to him, 'Captain Stives, you have a choice to make.' Tim said, 'Yes, sir. What is it?' And the Lt. Colonel said to Tim, 'You have to choose between your wife and the Army.' It seems I was not a good Army wife. I did not go to the wives' tea gatherings, or any of the other Army functions that were held on the post. I had a job and I was going to school, trying to finish my degree. Well, Tim made his decision. He chose me, and we are still together, getting ready for our 50th wedding anniversary."

Tim resigned from the active Army and went back to school on the GI Bill, earning an MBA from Rutgers University in 1975. He remained in the National Guard and Reserves for another 16 years while pursuing his career on Wall Street. Tim retired as a Lt. Colonel in 1991.

When Tim comes back to Fairless Hills, he often visits the grave of his high school classmate, Ed Beers, a Marine who was killed in Vietnam in May 1968.

"I think Tim does that because he really respected Eddie," Christine said. "Eddie was one of the guys who didn't wait for his draft notice. He volunteered for the Marines, knowing that he would probably end up in Vietnam."

Christine and Tim Stives are retired now and alternate between homes in Western Pa. and Florida. They can look back in their reflective moments and think about how that one year in their lives affected them.

"I think that year brought us closer," Christine Stives said. "It certainly made me appreciate Tim more. I was very grateful Tim came home because so many soldiers did not. You never forget that."

EXPOSED POSITION – B Battery, 2nd Battalion, 32nd Field Artillery, occupied a location on the northwest perimeter of Tay Ninh base camp, with an open area extending all the way out to the distant tree line. (Photo courtesy of Terry Banks)

CHAPTER TWELVE
Attack on B Battery

BY TERRY NAU

Every soldier stationed in a combat zone must wonder if and when his courage under fire will ever be tested. There is plenty of time to reflect on this possibility because down time is built into a combat soldier's schedule.

In an artillery battery, time can drag on. During the Vietnam War, a typical day for an artilleryman might consist of filling countless sand bags, fortifying bunkers, cleaning weapons and waiting for a fire mission. Incoming mortar rounds were almost a daily occurrence. Artillery soldiers generally worked eight hours on and eight hours off but they were always on call. Half of the four gun crews were up at night, firing harassment rounds at predesignated targets out in the bush. Half of the eight Fire Direction Control soldiers were on duty, manning the battalion radio net, on guard for a fire mission. Those two words – "fire mission!" -- would spring soldiers into action on the guns and in the FDC.

Artillerymen learned how to sleep lightly, and to recognize the sounds of incoming mortar fire during that semi-conscious state, while managing to block out the booming sounds of their unit's own heavy guns firing outgoing rounds into the night. And it could get very dark in Vietnam. Dark enough for enemy "sapper squads" to occasionally sneak through concertina wire and into camp.

Soldiers of B Battery, 2/32 artillery, would remember the night of May 22, 1968 for the rest of their lives. That was the night sapper squads breached the perimeter of Tay Ninh base camp. One sapper squad of three enemy soldiers got inside B Battery's perimeter and sneaked into the ammo bunker with the intent of blowing up the artillery shells stored inside. They went to work while American troops were distracted by incoming mortars and rocket propelled grenades. It didn't take long to distinguish these sounds from a random mortar attack.

Three of the B Battery soldiers reluctantly agreed to share their memories of that attack for this book. Gary Hove, Mike Jarrett and Terry Banks all worked in FDC. Jarrett and Hove were on duty when the attack began. Banks was trying to get some sleep over in his hooch, located around 30 yards from the battery's guns, ammo bunker and FDC outpost.

Gary Hove was not a typical enlisted soldier. By the time this six-foot tall Californian arrived in the Republic of Vietnam in August 1967, he was 23 years old, schooled in college for four years, and well trained by the Army in the skill set of heavy weapons. Most of his fellow soldiers in B Battery were three or four years younger. Hove assumed a natural role of leader and eventually became section chief of FDC for B Battery.

"I had been trained on an M60 machine gun and the M2 (50-caliber)," Hove admitted in the spring of 2019, nearly 51 years after he came home from Vietnam. "I was on duty at the FDC bunker when the attack came that night. Fortunately, we had an extra M60 and ammo in the FDC. I picked up the gun and the ammo and rushed outside. I was part of the reaction team, which included three other soldiers. When they got near the ammo bunker, they were immediately fired upon. I took position on the ground and set up the M60 on its bipod. I could see the silhouettes of the enemy. One of our guys was firing on the ammo bunker and I told him to stop because his rounds might set off something inside. What we didn't know was the sappers had already been inside and started 'cooking' the powder charges."

Everything happened quickly in the sudden chaos of war. Hove managed to kill two of the sappers with machine gun fire. Mike Jarrett killed the third with his M14 rifle. The ammo bunker finally exploded, sending soldiers flying into the air, their ear drums temporarily shattered by the devastating noise of steel projectiles igniting. At the end of the hour-long attack, three members of B Battery had been killed – Corporal Joseph Czajkowski, Corporal Clair Richey Jr. and Sgt. Philip Smith Jr. The enemy also used satchel charges to destroy a 175-mm gun and an 8-inch howitzer along with a M548 ammo carrier.

The sapper attack was part of a coordinated assault on Tay Ninh base camp, which was home to units of the 25th Infantry Division and the 2/32 artillery battalion. Both Headquarters Company and B Battery of the 2/32 were hit right away. According to battle reports, the base camp received 200 rounds of enemy mortar fire along with approximately 30 RPG rounds and 10 rockets. The attack began with heavy mortar fire and a few rockets. Some small arms fire kept American soldiers pinned down. The enemy also tossed hand grenades and set up satchel charges as they probed B Battery's perimeter and broke through not long after midnight.

"I still remember that night," Hove recalled. "May 22 was my dad's birthday. When the bunker exploded, I was thrown 30 feet in the air. Still, I was very lucky. Both my ear drums were ruined. I took a small piece of shrapnel in my knee but it could have been much worse. The real heroes were the three soldiers who died that night. I remember pulling one of them away from the ammo bunker. He was so bloody, I couldn't get a good grip. He kept slipping out of my hands. I got him over to a safe place but I never realized he had died until I went to the Vietnam Wall and read the gentleman's name many years later."

ON THE JOB – Fire Direction chief Gary Hove was part of the reaction team that neutralized a sapper squad attack on B Battery, 2/32 artillery, on the night of May 22, 1968. (Photo courtesy of Gary Hove)

157

Hove has lived with the memory of that night ever since. The surprise attack perpetrated by enemy sappers, and the ensuing explosion of the battery's ammo dump, will stick forever in his mind. Killing two enemy soldiers is not what keeps him up at night.

"They were either going to kill me or my friends," he said. "I had no choice. There were no other options but to kill them."

Nobody was really surprised that B Battery had been hit with a sapper attack. The battery's position was very much exposed on the northwest perimeter of the camp.

"There were a couple bunkers out in front of us," Hove recalled, "but the engineers came in one day and took them down. You could see all the way out to the tree line."

Mike Jarrett, who was on duty that night with Gary Hove, wrote down his own story many years later and agreed to publish his recollections only after much time had elapsed. Here is Mike's account, in his own words:

MIKE JARRETT

I was 19 years old and had been "in country" since February. I was working as a chart operator and radio telephone operator out of the Fire Direction Center. Gary Hove was our Section Chief. When the attack started, it was just mortars. We had been getting a lot of incoming fire over the last month. I thought it was just another mortar attack. Then the small arms and RPGs started. My guess was the mortars made us keep our heads down while the RPGs took out the guard bunkers.

Sappers came into our battery area. One of our M60s got turned around on us. Gary said we were under attack. He took an M60 and went out of the FDC to the left. I went out to the right with my M14. I was pretty clueless about what was going on. I couldn't see Gary but I could see his tracers going out between two of the guns.

The ammo bunker in front of me caught fire. I saw a guy crawling out of the window. I thought it was one of our guys at first and rushed forward to help him, only to see it was one of the enemy sappers. Holy Crap! I shot him. Then I turned around and went back to my post beside the FDC bunker. I had made it to the corner when the ammo bunker blew.

158

I think my last couple of steps saved my life. I heard later there were around 90 shells of 175 projectiles and powders in the bunker.

I remember flying through the air and landing on my face and elbows. Then it was like being in a hail storm – only the hail was hot metal. That was the only time my flak jacket served as anything other than a pillow.

I made it back across the road to our hooches (living quarters). I met Phil Clemente, another FDC guy, and he asked where Gary was. I told him he was still across the road. We went back over to find him. Gary wore glasses which he had lost when the ammo bunker blew. He also couldn't hear because of the explosion. Phil tackled Gary and got him back across the road.

I met the Battery Commander and another guy named Fox. The BC said we needed to clear the area. He took my M14 rifle, gave me his 45-caliber pistol and said he would cover us. Crawling across the ground to the other gun positions, I came across the enemy soldier I had shot. He was burnt pretty badly by the explosion. Holy Crap No. 2.

The ammo bunker was just a hole now. The 175 gun had been destroyed. The M548 (ammo carrier) looked like it had been crushed by a giant. I heard they found the gun driver's hatch over by the PX. My heart was in my throat, big time. I wanted this over. We found one guy in a Conex (large storage container) by the last gun. He wasn't hurt but I said I was taking him to the medics. The area was cleared as far as I was concerned.

There is no doubt that absent Gary Hove's action, the sappers would have gotten more of our guns. There was only one hero that night and it was Gary. He did everything right. I believe he received a Bronze Star for Valor and a Purple Heart.

***

TERRY BANKS joined B Battery in April 1968.

"I was working in the timber industry back home in Louisiana in the summer of 1967. My draft notice came in August. A month later, I was in the Army at Ft Polk and six months after that, I came to B

Battery in Tay Ninh. I had been trained at Ft Sill for FDC but since I had decent mechanical skills I was put in charge of the generators as well as working in FDC. I was just learning the ropes in early May when the mortar attacks stepped up. Also we were hearing about enemy activity on Nui Ba Den Mountain. On May 12, we listened over the battalion radio net as the Special Forces unit along with personnel from several other units on top of mountain were overrun by a sizeable force. I think the combined loss was 24 guys that night. We could hear their radio calls asking for artillery support until their communications were destroyed by the enemy. I think our guns fired a lot of rounds in support of those guys but they were up there by themselves. It was bad. I won't ever forget hearing the RTO asking for more help."

The Tet Offensive had occurred three months earlier, an attempt by the enemy to create chaos all over South Vietnam, but American troops had withstood the assault. By May 1968, the North Vietnamese Army, infiltrating from nearby Cambodia, was beginning to focus on Tay Ninh base camp, and the artillery units in separate fire bases that were giving them headaches all over the II Field Forces region. It didn't take a genius to know an attack might be coming on B Battery.

"Our position was pretty exposed," Banks recalled, thinking of B Battery's location near the west gate, where Headquarters Company of the 2/32 was also attacked on the night of May 22. "We took a few mortar rounds almost every day during my first month there but the rounds usually missed most critical targets. I think the enemy was aiming at the 25th Infantry post next door to us as well as our guns. Some nights, we would get reports in FDC of 'VC in the wire.' Or maybe we would see trip flares set off by movement outside our perimeter. We knew there were 'visitors' out there, testing us.

"On the night of May 22, I was off-duty, like a lot of the guys. We were in our sleeping quarters. In case of an attack, my job was to team up with Sgt. O'Malley and another soldier whose name I have forgotten and man the 81 millimeter mortar. Our job was to fire illumination rounds in case of a night-time attack. The best I can remember, the attack began around midnight. We could hear a lot of incoming rounds going off. Sgt. O'Malley, myself and the other unnamed soldier went over to the 81 mortar to fire illumination but our first round never came out of the tube. The tube was too dirty! So we had to take the round out and swab the tube. Then the second round detonated at extremely high altitude so we gave up on the mortar. The best I can remember, that is about the time our ammo bunker was blown up. That was the biggest explosion I have ever seen. I lost hearing in my left ear from the blast. I feel very fortunate. I'm still amazed that anyone in close proximity to the blast survived. After we regained our composure, we looked around and saw two of our guns destroyed as well as the ammo bunker."

Banks continued his narrative, the words flowing quickly as he remembered the night-time attack from 51 years earlier.

"I think Sgt. O'Malley, the other soldier and myself worked our way over near the FDC and took a position behind a wall of used powder canisters that had been filled with dirt and were used for a barrier wall. I actually cannot remember if I engaged any enemy or not. Due to the low light conditions it was hard to make a positive identity. I could hear our machine gun still firing. We found out later that was one of our FDC guys, Gary Hove. He did an outstanding job that night. The attack might have lasted an hour before it stopped and we could sweep the area. We had three KIAs and several wounded soldiers. I remember we found the body of Joe Czajkowski near the mess hall. He had been hit by a lot of shrapnel. Joe was a big guy, a good guy, and putting him on a stretcher was another thing I will never forget.

"I was kind of in shock after the attack. The ammo bunker was a hole in the ground. We lost two of our artillery guns and three of our men. I had been in country around six weeks at this point and now I knew what the war looked like up close."

Banks still had 10 months to serve after that harrowing night in May 1968.

"Later on in my tour, I was asked to serve as a radio operator for Lt. Jim Owens. We were assigned to provide artillery support to an ARVN infantry unit. We left Tay Ninh and choppered into a cold landing zone. Not real sure where. That was the first time I saw a helicopter troop insertion up close. I took some concern at all the firing from the gunships during the insertion. I did not settle down until the helicopters left the area and things became quiet. The dirt in the bomb craters that we took cover in was warm from very recent bombing and artillery fire. Another dose of war up close. I am not sure how long we stayed out in the bush but I do remember we walked into a friendly village with a small airstrip and were picked up by a Fairchild 123 aircraft that carried us to Cu Chi. I do not remember any more details on getting back to Tay Ninh.

"When I came back to the States, I had a little less than 120 days on my hitch so I qualified for an early out. I immediately took advantage."

MAP MAN – Terry Banks spent a lot of time plotting targets on the FDC map during his stint in Vietnam. (Photo courtesy of Terry Banks)

The war went into the recesses of Terry Banks' brain for the next three decades.

"I did not talk about the war in depth with anyone for least 30 years," he admitted in the spring of 2019. "Lately, I have been reading some books on the war. I was really kind of a naïve kid when I went into the Army. Kind of feel bad about the things we did to that country. I have some memories that will never leave me."

Fortunately, Terry Banks came home to friends and family who supported him during the difficult transition back to the real world.

"After I returned home to Louisiana, I was treated very well by my friends and relatives," Banks wrote in an email during May 2019. "No one had anything negative to say about any of the troops that served in Vietnam War. This was a blessing. I worked in the offshore oil fields for a few years. Then I got into inland and ocean transportation for mining and heavy construction equipment. I worked domestic and international trade until I retired in March 2017. I was very close to Vietnam several times in my career but never had a desire to go back and visit".

***

CAPTAIN GARY PERRYMAN, who would take over as commander of B Battery in October 1968, began his Vietnam tour of duty in June 1968 with the 23rd Artillery Group headquarters in Phu Loi. One of his first tasks was reading the after-action report of the May 22 attack in search of errors that were made and needed to be corrected.

"Most of the people on duty had left their personal weapons back in the sleeping areas," Perryman admitted in a January 2018 email exchange with the author. "That was also where the-off duty people were sleeping. When I took command we had larger bunkers built that could keep all soldiers near the guns with their weapons. This made fighting back much easier. The soldiers (on May 22) did not have the necessary means to fight the sappers. Gary Hove and Mike Jarrett and a few other soldiers did a great job once in action. Being in the sleeping hooches at the time of the attack was a problem. After I took over B

Battery, we stressed light discipline (turning out the lights) heavily. The darkness caused incoming mortars to miss the battery area more often."

B Battery's location on the edge of base camp made the unit totally vulnerable to a sapper attack.

"The battery was overlooked by about 2,000 yards of rice paddies to the west," Perryman noted. "We could watch ox carts on the far side come down a road. Often we watched them to see if they stopped near trees along the road. Maybe they were moving ammo, to be used on us."

***

The attack on B Battery was one of the most destructive events of the war for the 2/32 artillery battalion during its seven years in the Republic of Vietnam. Three soldiers died within an hour, an ammo dump was blown up by enemy sappers, and a 175 gun disabled with satchel charges. Not to mention the disabled M548 ammo carrier. The battery's exposed position made an attack almost inevitable. If not for the reactive responses of several soldiers, the damage could have been a lot worse.

Specialist Fifth Class Hove had been in other dangerous camps during his time in Vietnam, which began in August 1967. When asked about his first seven months in the war zone, Hove instead harkened back to his final days in the U.S. before heading to the Republic of Vietnam.

"I had a 30-day leave before coming to Vietnam," the California native said in early 2019. "I broke my left ankle a week before I was supposed to report. I was hiking with my girlfriend. The hospital put me into a walking cast. The Army, in its wisdom, did not delay my departure date. They had a quota to fill. When I got to Vietnam, they put me in a hospital for three or four days and then the cast came off. I just laced on my combat boots and joined my unit, B Battery, which was stationed at Sou Da at the time. We were hit with mortar attacks many times. At first, my job was to serve as a liaison between our Executive officer and a Vietnamese 105 battery that was nearby. I spoke enough French to get by. I would try to communicate in French with the South Vietnamese officer. He did not speak English and we couldn't speak Vietnamese. French was our middle ground. It was tough in the middle of an attack to translate my thoughts from English to French but I did it."

Not long after that, Hove became a member of FDC, plotting targets for B Battery's guns to fire at. It was an easier job than working on the guns. Cannoneers lifted heavy projectiles and were exposed to mortar fire during live missions while FDC worked in relatively safe bunkers.

When Gary Hove came home from Vietnam in late August of 1968, his problems were just beginning.

"I went over the edge," he admitted. "Lots of bars. Motorcycles. I went through a couple of marriages pretty quickly. Eventually, I came back to my faith in God, but only after I attempted suicide. I was no different than a lot of guys who came home and struggled. You wanted to end it all. I look at Vietnam now as a crossroads in my life. If I hadn't come home, my daughter and her children would not exist. I was raised in a Lutheran church. Now we go to a non-denominational church. I met a good woman who became my wife. She gets upset when I talk about the war because she worries, I guess, that the bad memories will return, but I have been working on recovering for 30 years. She is very positive and makes me stronger. I would like to set up a ministry to help other vets who struggle with the effects of fighting in a war zone."

Mike Jarrett took a different path than most Vietnam vets. He stayed in the Army.

"I extended my (Vietnam) tour for six months and re-enlisted there," Jarrett wrote in an email during late May of 2019. "I went on to become the FDC section chief. After my tour ended, I went back to Fort Sill where I met my future wife. Two years later, after a trip to Fort Bliss and Vietnamese Language School, I was back in Vietnam on an advisory team. As the war stood down and the advisory teams went away, I spent my last three months working for Brigadier General John

McGiffert, the Deputy Commander of Military Region III. When I was leaving country, he asked what he could do for me. I requested an assignment to Alaska. I managed to stay there for seven years before my next assignment took me to Fort Carson, Colorado. It was there that some old injuries forced me to get out of combat arms. I had the rank of E7 at this point. I was reclassified to Personnel Senior Sergeant. I managed to get one more assignment in Alaska at Fort Wainwright.

"I had been in the Army 21 years when orders came down for an assignment in Washington, D.C. With three children, two of them in high school, I decided to retire from the Army. I was a Master Sergeant by then. I went to work for the Alaska Fire Service for another 21 years before I retired again. I finished up as a Human Resource Officer for the U.S. Fish and Wildlife Service, Alaska Region. I am now a great grandfather! I ride my motorcycle with the Combat Veterans Motorcycle Association and do what I can to help other veterans. Life is good, and I am blessed."

TEAM EFFORT – Members of Operation Song, mingling with Army veterans at a 2018 reunion, have made it their mission to create music that promotes healing. (Photo by Terry Nau)

CHAPTER THIRTEEN
Healing Through Music

BY TERRY NAU

When my Vietnam War buddies decided to hold our 2018 reunion in Chattanooga, the hosts, Dennie and Marti Wolfgang, worked hard to make this occasion a special event. After all, this reunion would mark the 50th anniversary of the combat experience for many in our group. We were all members of A Battery, 2/32 artillery, which carried the nickname, "Proud Americans."

Marti Wolfgang enlisted her friends to embroider patriotic quilts for each of the 21 soldiers on our reunion list. These would be presented at a final dinner on Saturday evening, Sept. 22, 2018.

Marti had another surprise for us, besides the quilts. She hired a group of songwriters who are on a mission to spread emotional healing through their music. "Operation Song" works with combat veterans, policemen, emergency care technicians and others who have experienced trauma in their lives.

"Dennie and I first heard Operation Song perform in 2016 at a 4th of July celebration hosted by Chattanooga Pops," Marti Wolfgang recalled. "Don Goodman and Steve Dean shared 'Chattanooga Rain,' a song written by Lori Wyatt, the wife of one of five members of the military killed during an attack on a Navy Reserve Center in Chattanooga on July 16, 2015. That put Operation Song on our radar screen.

"In April 2017, Don and Steve performed songs at the annual Chattanooga Volunteer Awards Luncheon that we attended. (Dennie volunteers at the VA Clinic.) I was so touched by their songs that I approached them about creating songs with our guys at the 50th reunion we would be hosting in September 2018. They were eager to work with us. They put me in touch with Bobbi Standifer, their Chattanooga Program Coordinator.

169

"In October 2017, I met with the Operation Song team to determine how they could be part of our reunion," Marti added. "They shared a weekend workshop format that would work. We firmed up the date and the details. In August 2018, we met once again to finalize details for their role in our reunion. Between meetings, I had numerous phone calls with Bobbi and Don to facilitate the planning. Lee Waters, a veteran and an Operation song team member, not to mention a professional photographer, volunteered to take photographs of our quilt ceremony. Al Jarvis, another veteran and Operation Song Team Member, volunteered to provide the sound expertise for our Saturday night dinner and the performing of our new songs."

Not everyone was on board right away with this idea of songwriters interviewing veterans about their war experiences. I had my doubts. A few months earlier, Marti asked me what I thought about Operation Song. Would this interaction work with our group of war veterans? Having no idea what Operation Song had already accomplished in its six years of existence, I expressed a few reservations, noting that some Vietnam vets don't like to be pressed too far on what they saw during the war. Marti shrugged me off, knowing that Operation Song had already achieved great success in its mission to help heal wounded warriors.

I would later learn that Operation Song, which originated in Nashville, had written over 400 songs since 2012, working with veterans whose service dated back to World War II and up through the current wars.

On its website, Operation Song defines itself this way: "Our mission is to empower veterans, active duty military, and their families to tell their stories through the process of songwriting."

And so it came to pass that on Friday night, Sept. 21, our group of Vietnam veterans and wives met the musicians on a permanently docked barge located on the Tennessee River, and got to know some of them as they performed an impromptu concert. There were five musicians in the group, ranging from 40 years young to around our age, in the early 70s. We drank a beer or two with them and shared something of each other.

On Saturday morning, we got up bright and early and met with the songwriters, pairing off three vets with each musician, and then retreated to hotel rooms for the songwriting process. This was the part we veterans worried about in advance. There was no reason to be wary. The musicians were very respectful and only wanted to hear the basics of our experience so that they could create a unique song relating to what we told them in conversations.

Nine hours after the songwriting process began, these musicians got up on a stage in the hotel's ballroom and sang their songs. We were blown away. They sang songs about "Ho Chi Minh Hell," and "Friendly Fire," about being 19 years old and stuck in Vietnam. They created a song about Captain Babb, our battery commander who lost both legs in a mortar attack on Sept. 17, 1968. Fifty years and five days later, Capt. Babb heard this song played to him over a phone, and realized his soldiers had never forgotten him.

With permission from Operation Song, here are the lyrics to the five songs that were created at our reunion, with a short introduction that explains the interview process.

CAPTAIN BABB

(Created through the memories of Carl Miller, Mike Neisius, Chuck Rosenblum and the talents of songwriter Jerry Vandiver.)

Don Babb served as our battery commander for less than two months before a mortar attack on Sept. 17, 1968 killed two infantry officers standing next to him and took off our Captain's legs at the knees. His soldiers never saw him again. Over the years, each of us at some point wondered how Captain Babb's life turned out. Fortunately, we found Don Babb earlier in 2018 and arranged a Skype video phone call for the Friday afternoon of our reunion weekend. Captain Babb was talkative and eased the awkwardness for his former soldiers. This phone conversation set the stage for what would follow on a special weekend.

That night, Operation Song artist Jerry Vandiver listened to some of the guys talk about their phone call with Captain Babb. He met with Carl and Mike and Chuck on Saturday morning and they collaborated on this tribute to our former leader, who lives out near Lake Tahoe and devoted his life to helping others who had lost a leg or arm, not just in the military but in the real world.

171

Don heard that song later in our reunion weekend. He shared it with some of his friends and his sons. Here was a piece of music that spoke of his soldiers' appreciation for what he had accomplished in those six weeks of duty in Vietnam to make their lives safer.

CAPTAIN BABB

He was all Army, out of the Point
In country on his second tour
Stepped off the chopper
Took a long look,
Said we've got work to do
"So get your shit together
And your head out of your ass"
That's how we got to know
Captain Babb

We worked eight hours on,
Eight hours off, 24/7, you know
We had a calendar,
Marking each day, till we got home
But we got our shit together
And our head out of our ass
'Cause we'd do anything
For Captain Babb

Ya, he cared about his men
Time and again
And kept us all in one piece
We couldn't count all the mortar rounds
But I truly believe, we're all here today
Because of Captain Babb

It was getting dark, just about 8,
When the shells started coming down
And I'll never forget

When the smoke cleared
Captain took a round
We think it was Carl
Who called the chopper in
And yelled for a medivac
On the stretcher was the last time
We saw Captain Babb.

Ya, he cared about his men
Time and again
And he kept us all in one piece
We couldn't count all the mortar rounds
But I truly believe, we're all here today
Because of Captain Babb

He's in good spirits,
With his gift of gab
It's abundantly clear, we all still revere
Captain Babb.

FRIENDLY FIRE

(Created through the memories of Larry Bond, Mel Major, and Dennie Wolfgang along with the talents of song writers Steve Dean and Don Goodman.)

In Vietnam, an artillery soldier's worst fear was a shell that fell in the wrong place and wounded or killed one of our soldiers out in the countryside. Fortunately, these occurrences were very rare, but on a dark night in 1969, a gun sight on one of A Battery's artillery cannons became defective, perhaps from overuse.

This was a nightmare that Dennie Wolfgang in particular has dealt with for more than 50 years. It was not his fault but he heard the frantic radio call for "Check fire" and learned not long afterwards that a soldier had died.

For this songwriting session, Dennie, Larry Bond and Mel Major contributed their thoughts to songwriters Steve Dean and Don

Goodman. The song begins with a call for artillery support from an infantry unit. Within a couple of minutes, an artillery shell was on its way to the target. But it fell short.

This song is haunting to hear performed. It speaks to a not uncommon occurrence of friendly fire that can happen to infantry units that cross each other in the bush, or from a plane flying over the soldiers, or from the artillery. Friendly Fire. As the songwriters ask at the end of the song, "Lord, why would you call it friendly fire?"

FRIENDLY FIRE

X-ray Tango
Went Bango
27/67 Battery A
Put Hell in the pocket
Of someone in the jungle
15 miles away

The shell went whistlin'
And we sat listening
To the radio
Praying we'd hear
'Fire for Effect'
'Not Check Fire! ... OOH NOOO!

Friendly Fire
We just took someone's life
Mothers and young widows cryin'
I hear them every night
Left a crater and a funeral pyre
And they called it Friendly Fire

Here they come, one by one
Tears streaming down their faces
From Michigan, California,
Tennessee and Texas

In the blink of an eye
We changed their lives
Turned their dreams into screams

Friendly Fire
We just took someone's life
Mothers and young widows cryin'
I hear them every night
A crater and a funeral pyre
And they called it Friendly Fire

50 years have come and gone
And still the war goes on and on
Every night when I close my eyes
I hear 'Check Fire!'

Friendly Fire
We just took someone's life
I hear them every night
A crater and a funeral pyre
And they called it Friendly Fire
Lord, Why-y-y-y would you call it
Friendly Fire?

PROUD AMERICANS, 19 YEARS OLD

(Created through the memories of Bill Kimball, Bob McLean, Larry Smith and the talents of musician Will Nance.)

The most common age for a young soldier during the Vietnam War Era was 19. That's when your draft notice showed up in the mail box for most of us. If you enlisted, the age could be 17, 18 or 19. The Army trained soldiers for four months. After a month's leave back home with family, many of these soldiers headed straight to the war zone. Often still teenagers, they had little idea what kind of insanity lay ahead.

Bill Kimball, Bob McLean and Larry Smith all fit that age timeline. And when they met with singer-songwriter Will Nance, their

175

remembrances focused on the innocence they took into combat. "Proud Americans, USA-born, some came from the city, some raised on a farm." That was the American military in the 1960s, heavily weighted with teenage combat veterans, working hard every day, and taking pride in the jobs they performed.

PROUD AMERICANS, 19 YEARS OLD

Nineteen years old,
Nineteen sixty six
Some drafted, some enlisted
Noth'n but kids
Thrown out into the boonies
Of Vietnam
Didn't take long to became a man

Pour'n concrete, building hooches
Shoot'n guns day and night
No run'n water,
No flip'n on the lights,
Bugs and rats and snakes, yeah
They were everywhere
But old Rudolph the red-nosed
Caribou brought us some
Christmas Beer

Proud Americans, USA born
Some came from the city,
Some raised on a farm
Side by side, arm in arm,
Do'n duty to our country
Letters from home
Made us all feel better
Til Old Joe
Got that Dear John letter
Tween that and a cigarette

He was try'n hard to light
The rockets and mortars,
We were trying to stay alive

Proud Americans, USA born
Some came from the city
Some raised on a farm
Side by side, arm in arm
Do'n duty to our country
Thirty five years later,
Got on the Internet
Left my name and number
Heard from another vet
Led to a reunion
Not know'n what to expect
And old stories that we told
There was laughter
There were tears
Things we hadn't
Talked about in years
Proud Americans, USA born
Some came from the city,
Some raised on a farm
Side by side, arm in arm
Do'n duty to our country
Proud Americans, USA born

HO CHI MINH HELL

(Created through the memories of Kenneth Barbian, Tony Hoehner and Terry Nau along with the talents of musician Rusty Tabor.)

During the songwriting interview, Rusty Tabor settled on telling the veterans' stories through the cadence of an artillery fire mission. Our unit's radio call sign was Hercules 59. And nine on the radio was pronounced 'niner' to distinguish it from the number five. "Number

One Adjust" referred to a command to the gun crew from the Fire Direction Center. Deflection meant direction and quadrant referred to the elevation of the gun's tube.

Tabor came up with the refrain about "infantry needs artillery." The "bird dogs" in the clear referred to forward observers in small planes who had spotted the target, relayed coordinates, and moved out of the firing line. The rest of the song just took off. Rusty kept asking the former artillerymen questions, and we provided answers that mentioned Ho Chi Minh, the Black Virgin Mountain and dead soldiers going back to Dover, Delaware (because he needed a word to rhyme with "over"). We described our unit's journey over the first eight months of 1968, from the Tet Offensive and our visit to Cu Chi and then over to our final encampment around seven miles north of the Black Virgin Mountain, where we fired shell after shell, and dodged mortar attacks.

CREATIVE SONGWRITER – Rusty Tabor wrote the lyrics and then sang his song, "Ho Chi Minh Hell," to Vietnam War veterans. (Photo by Terry Nau)

178

We broke up after about three hours and Rusty went to his room and came up with this song. I can only speak for myself but hearing Rusty sing his song on Saturday night was just so touching, to hear a young man in his 40s putting our Vietnam experience to music, and singing his words in haunting fashion. The song has become a keepsake for me. I listen to it at odd times, as a diversion from real life. "Ho Chi Minh Hell" takes me back in time, back to when we were all 20 years old again, doing a complicated job, helping our infantry soldiers from long distance. 1968 mostly seems very far away but this song brings it back for me.

HO CHI MINH HELL
Hercules Five Niner
Number One Adjust
Deflection 3200
Quadrant 361
Infantry needs artillery
The bird dogs are in the clear
We've got men pinned in the combat zone
They're the reason why we're here

We're 100 young men
Thrown into a Ho Chi Minh Hell
At the foot of Black Virgin Mountain
We sent shell after shell
We're red and yellow, black and white
The Proud Americans
Got your back tonight
Here's to the heroes
Who only made it back to Dover
Five Niner Over

The Tet Offensive took us
To the Cu Chi side of war
A few months later, helpless,
We couldn't save the Signal Corps

Then 42 straight days of mortars
Took us to the edge
Some took to our knees
One took Captain Babb's legs

We're a 100 young men
Thrown into a Ho Chi Minh Hell
At the foot of Black Virgin Mountain
We sent shell after shell
We're red and yellow, black and white
The Proud Americans
Got your back tonight
Here's to the heroes
Who only made it back to Dover
Five Niner Over

The cannoneers
Were the backbone
The FDC the bridge
But when that fire mission
Call came in
We were one to the bitter end

We were just a 100 young men
Thrown into a Ho Chi Minh Hell
At the foot of Black Virgin Mountain
We sent shell after shell
And we were red and yellow
We were black and white
The Proud Americans got your back alright
Here's to the heroes
Who only made it back to Dover
Five Niner Over
Yeah, that big Freedom Bird
She's circling back around
Five Niner Out

FIRE IN THE HOLE

(Created through the memories of Jerry Granberg and Tom Preston, and the talents of Steve Dean and Don Goodman.)

This song touches on the subject of Survivors' Guilt that plagues many soldiers who have experienced combat. Why does one soldier die while another is spared? In a world turned upside down, where probing enemy soldiers attempt to break through concertina wire at night, and mortar attacks come with regularity, a state of adrenalin exists that is hard to turn off when the soldier finally goes home.

A Battery, 2/32 artillery, saw a lot of action in 1969-70. Its home base sat in the middle of nowhere, a sitting duck for the enemy. Fortunately, the base was heavily protected by Quad-50 machine guns on each corner, devastating enough to discourage full-scale attacks. Enemy sapper squads, three-man teams, would probe the wire long after the sun went down. American troops might wake up in the morning to see a body hung up in that wire, killed by gunfire or a claymore mine.

Jerry Granberg and Tom Preston spoke to songwriters Steve Dean and Don Goodman about their time in Vietnam. The resulting song describes perhaps the scariest episode for A Battery in its seven years of service during the Vietnam War.

FIRE IN THE HOLE

Firebase St. Barbara 1969
Isolation and danger
Bodies burning in the wire
That smell still lingers
For a Lieutenant from Colorado
For a Spec 4 from Texas
It's still welcome to the Alamo

That was 50 years ago
But it seems like yesterday
Twelve months of Hell
That just won't go away

Smoke, dust and shells
Still ringing in our ears
I hear Fire in the Hole
And Vietnam is here
Just when we thought
It couldn't get any worse, it did
Alpha Battery was used as bait
And we lost some real good men
When the shooting stopped
We were thankful
We weren't one of them
But when we came home
The guilt closed in
And we were different men
That was 50 years ago
But it seems like yesterday
Twelve months of Hell
That just won't go away
Smoke, dust and shells
Still ringing in our ears
I hear Fire in the Hole
And Vietnam is here – Ya
That was 50 years ago
But it seems like yesterday
Twelve months of Hell
That just won't go away
Smoke, dust and shells
Still ringing in our ears
I hear Fire in the Hole
And Vietnam is here – Ya
I hear Fire in the Hole ...

PROUD AMERICAN – Cannoneer Bill Van Eck paints new name on a 175 mm gun barrel. Van Eck earned a Bronze Star for his part in the Trung Lap rescue mission. (Photo courtesy of Bill Van Eck)

CHAPTER FOURTEEN
Trung Lap Rescue Mission

BY TERRY NAU

This rare episode of artillery soldiers rescuing an ambushed platoon of engineers occurred on January 13, 1966, just two months after the 2/32 battalion had arrived in the war zone. The 2/32 had spread out around the Saigon area, setting up temporary fire bases, while dodging occasional mortar and rocket attacks from the Viet Cong, who were masters of the hit-and-run style of warfare, having practiced their skills against the French after World War II ended.

American soldiers, frustrated by the enemy's tactics, were itching for a fight.

The Vietnam War, American phase, had hardly begun. In 1966, U.S. soldiers were still learning how to fight an enemy intent on conducting guerilla warfare, a non-traditional style of combat fought on the opposition's home turf. The VC mined roads at night. They staged ambushes and then fled into the bush after firing off a few rounds. Now you see them, now you don't.

"We were tired of being attacked almost daily by snipers, land mines and especially mortars," Specialist Fourth Class Bill Van Eck recalled in the winter of 2018-19. "We had been fighting a ghost."

Van Eck and his fellow C Battery soldiers drew closer to real action when the 2/32 was assigned to participate in Operation Crimp in early January 1966. They moved to a Special Forces camp outside the village of Trung Lap, not far from the larger village of Cu Chi, 40 miles northwest of Saigon. C Battery set up its perimeter next to a group of engineers from Charlie Company, 1st Engineer Battalion.

"I read somewhere, long after the war ended, that the object of Operation Crimp was to clear the area of tunnels," said Capt. Jay Franz, commander of Charlie Company. "At the time, so early in the war, we were not even aware the VC had tunnels dug all over the place. My unit was on line, right next to the artillery unit. Late on the afternoon of Jan. 13, I got a call reporting that a helicopter pilot had seen a short stretch of road that had apparently been mined. We were directed to check it out and clear any mines that were there. The stretch of road was very near our base camp, perhaps one or two kilometers away. Two of my platoons were at Trung Lap. I gave the mine-clearing mission to Lt. Joe Coppolo and his platoon. I decided to accompany them."

Van Eck and his artillery mates hung back in camp, waiting for any fire mission that might arise. They were eager to live up to the 2/32's unit nickname – Proud Americans.

"On the morning before that rescue mission," Van Eck recalled, "our mess kitchen needed water for cooking and washing pots and pans. The engineers had a water point set up outside the Special Forces compound. Mess Sergeant JD Gosnell and his close friend, Commo Sergeant Johnson, hooked up a trailer to the APC (armored personnel carrier) with a few Proud Americans as guards on the 50-caliber machine gun. Off we go to the water point. We started filling the trailer. Very soon, we saw some real water buffalo, a herd of them, heading in our direction. Someone from our detail noticed many of the water buffalo had extra pairs of human feet under them. JD called a march order (evacuation) while returning fire on the Viet Cong. That happened the day before the ambush."

Of course, this news spread among the soldiers at Trung Lap, including Capt. Franz's soldiers. The Captain sensed the Jan. 13 mission could feature contact with the enemy.

"We reached the area and dismounted from the dump trucks that brought us there," Franz said. "I was in my jeep with a brand new driver. Soon after we had all dismounted and started to sweep the road, we came under heavy fire from both sides of the road. I radioed for help. Helicopter gunships arrived quickly and laid down a lot of fire and – we thought – put the enemy out of commission. The gunships, with their mission accomplished, left the area and we continued to sweep the road. It became obvious that the 'disturbed' road was just to entice us into an ambush. There were no mines.

"As we started to return to our vehicles, the ambush was sprung again," Franz added. "This time there were no gunships to help us. They were either refueling or rearming. Typical of that area, the road was raised above the adjoining rice paddies. Lt. Coppolo's men responded beautifully and were returning fire, but the terrain provided us almost no cover."

It wasn't long before one of Lt. Coppolo's soldiers was wounded and appeared to be going into shock.

"Fearing that the soldier might die, we loaded him into the back of my jeep," Franz said. "Sgt. Ronald Riley got in the passenger seat. We proceeded to drive through moderately heavy fire out of the ambush zone and back to Trung Lap where we delivered the soldier to the aid station."

Capt. Franz and Sgt. Riley got back in the jeep and returned to the ambush. Remember, the ambush site was less than two kilometers away from base camp.

"After returning, I told Lt. Coppolo we would attempt to evacuate the area in the dump trucks, even though the men would be vulnerable to enemy fire as they mounted the slow-moving vehicles. Platoon Sergeant Baxter Carroll was on the driver's side running board of the first truck, encouraging men to board as the truck made its way out of the area. Less than 100 yards from the immediate ambush site, the truck was blown up by what today is called an IED (improvised explosive device). Sgt. Carroll was killed instantly and we had several other wounded soldiers.

"At the time of the explosion, I was standing by my jeep, using the radio to urge relief from some of the units in the camp. By the time they arrived, I had been wounded and was losing consciousness. I had been hit by two bullets. One went into my upper left arm and came out through my shoulder. The second bullet clipped my jaw and crushed a few teeth. I had a mouthful of broken teeth and blood."

Back at Trung Lap, Lt. Chuck Humphrey of Charlie Company had answered Capt. Franz's radio call for help. But who could he turn to?

"I had seen the PC that had a 50-caliber machine gun on top," Humphrey recalled. "I ran over to the soldiers and told them about the ambush and asked if they could help. They responded immediately. We rounded up five guys and off we went on the PC. Just a few artillery soldiers and myself."

Humphrey may not have remembered that two more artillery PCs packed with 12 soldiers followed his PC to the ambush site.

Bill Van Eck's version is more complete, from an artillery soldier's point of view.

"I was standing in the battery commander's tent, waiting to pick up the mail," Van Eck recalled. "Staff Sgt. Gosnell was there. He was a Korean War veteran. He had some papers for our battery commander to sign. That's when Lt. Humphrey came in, asking for help. I will never forget JD's eyes. He seemed to flash back to the Korean War. Right away, he told me to get the APCs and some men. We recruited 17 of our guys and three APCs."

Staff Sgt. Gosnell, SP4 Van Eck, PFC Guadalupe Perez, and Sgt. Burlap Cooper joined Humphrey on the first APC, which was driven by SP4 James Davies. The remaining artillery soldiers jumped on the other two APCs and headed out to the ambush site. Gosnell, a 35-year-old Army veteran, manned the 50-caliber machine gun located on top of the vehicle. This was the first serious action the troops around him were seeing.

"When we got to the ambush site," Humphrey said, "we jumped off the APC. Lt. Coppolo's platoon was spread out along the road, which had a lot of heavy shrubbery that made it a perfect ambush site for the VC. I got briefed on the situation by Sgt. Riley. He told me about Captain Franz being wounded. I went over and saw the Captain and he was in shock, drifting in and out of consciousness. I could see the whites of his eyes. We needed to get him back to Trung Lap as fast as possible. So we lowered the ramp of the PC and carried Capt. Franz inside. Two of the artillery guys stayed behind as the enemy was still spraying our area."

Van Eck and Perez took up a position near Capt. Franz and began firing into the thick bush used as cover by the enemy. Bullets were flying back and forth. The remaining two APCs set up a position across the road from the ambush site.

"Staff Sgt. Gosnell opened up with his 50-caliber machine gun and the rest of us fired our M-14s," Van Eck recalled. "I had reached the commander first and observed that he was out cold. PFC Perez and I took up our position a few feet away from Capt. Franz and tried to shield the rescue operation. The firing was extremely heavy. As we continued to fire, I was able to keep one eye on the rescue and the other on the Viet Cong to our front.

"We watched six or eight men, some who were wounded, and others who were helping the wounded, load themselves into the APC," Van Eck said. "I called to Perez, 'Let's go!' "

But the APC left without the two artillery soldiers. They quickly joined up with members of Lt. Coppolo's platoon who were still engaged with the enemy.

"Time passed and the shooting began to slow down," Van Eck said. "I guess 20 to 30 minutes went by. A Huey helicopter came in at tree top level and made one pass, shooting up the enemy position. By this time, the enemy had gone into hiding."

In the lull that followed, the soldiers made a break for the convoy's two dump trucks. Van Eck and Perez joined them. During this mad dash, Van Eck and Perez spotted Captain Franz's disabled jeep, pulled it out of a hole, and jumped in. They drove the jeep back to Trung Lap, trailing the dump trucks.

"Perez got the jeep started and within a few minutes we were safe behind friendly lines," Van Eck said. "I sat in the back, firing in the direction of the enemy. We picked up two engineers on the road back to Trung Lap. I believe this was the first rescue mission of its kind during U.S. participation in the Vietnam War."

Gosnell, Cooper and SP4 Bogan were awarded Bronze Stars with valor for their actions. Van Eck would be honored with a Bronze Star for his efforts in 2002, thanks to a supporting affidavit from Gosnell that described his actions during the rescue mission.

However, not everyone agreed with the idea of an impromptu rescue mission.

"We accomplished our mission without any Proud Americans getting wounded," Van Eck recalled. "But when we returned to camp, we got an ass-chewing. All of our officers had been away at a battalion meeting and were not consulted in the decision to rescue those ambushed soldiers."

The spontaneous reaction to Capt. Franz's call for help seemed like the right thing to do but some feathers were ruffled when enlisted soldiers began making decisions on the fly.

"Sgt. Gosnell was so angry, he asked to be transferred to his old job at the Officer's Club in Saigon," Van Eck remembered. "The transfer was granted. They wanted the rest of us to pay for ammo clips that had been used in the rescue. Lt. Humphrey heard about this and came over with a box of brand new ammo clips, barged into the Battery Commander's tent, and dropped them on the First Sergeant's desk. He started yelling at the BC and First Sergeant, asking them 'What the hell are you guys doing? If it wasn't for your men, we would have taken large losses!'

"I never forgot how red First Sergeant Gildernick's face got," Van Eck said, 53 years later. "He didn't say anything except 'Case dismissed.'"

Things got worse on the night of Jan. 13 as Trung Lap base camp came under heavy mortar fire. Three members of C Battery were wounded and subsequently awarded Purple Hearts (PFC Edward Thomas, Sgt. August Kessel and SP4 Roy Bryant).

"Our tent had over 180 shrapnel holes in it the next morning," Van Eck remembered.

J.D. GOSNELL
Veteran of two wars

Gosnell, in a supporting letter for Van Eck's Bronze Star application written 28 years later from his Arkansas home, recalled that day's battle.

"You may or may not know, I was transferred out of the battalion after an ambush by the VC at Trung Lap," Gosnell wrote. "They killed a couple engineers who were out looking for a better source of water for the 32nd Artillery. A young Lieutenant drove into the ambush area, looking to get the soldiers out. We got 16 of our guys on to APCs and went out to help them. I neglected to secure permission for us to go along.

"When we arrived in the area, we were met with intense fire from mortars and small arms," Gosnell continued. "I got that big 50-caliber on top of the PC I was on and returned fire. Then we loaded the wounded and took them to the aid station. I pulled out my canteen and saw the bottom had been shot out. My magazine pouch had also been hit and I couldn't fasten the belt. The male end had been shot off. I had not been that scared since October 1952 when I got hit in Korea on Hill 633."

Those are the memories of soldiers recalling this battle more than 50 years later. Maybe we would be better served to hear Sgt. Gosnell's sworn affidavit taken on Nov. 22, 1999 as he advocated for Bill Van Eck to receive a Bronze Star.

Here is the affidavit, in Gosnell's words:

"On or about Jan. 13, 1966, at the Trung Lap Special Forces Compound, Republic of Vietnam, at approximately 1200 to 1300 hours, I was near the main command post for C Battery, 2/32 Field Artillery. At that time, Lt. Fowler C. Humphrey, from C Company, 1st Engineers Battalion, 1st Infantry Division, came running by and announced that C Company's commander was just wounded in an ambush on the main road into Trung Lap. A call for volunteers was made, and within 5 minutes, 17 men volunteered to man three armored personnel carriers and help in the rescue of the wounded commander.

"I jumped into an APC with Lt. Humphrey, SP4 William Van Eck, PFC Guadalupe Perez, SSG William Douglas and a driver whose name I cannot remember at this time. Our APC proceeded through the outer gate of the compound until we reached the ambushed convoy with the wounded commander's jeep at the front of the convoy. On the way to the ambush site, our APC took gunfire several times. When we reached the ambush site, the convoy was taking heavy gunfire and there were many Engineers either wounded or killed. My APC proceeded to the front of the convoy where the wounded commander's jeep was located. The other APCs took up positions on the side of the road.

"The wounded commander's jeep was in a large mortar hole when my APC approached it. As my APC approached the jeep, I opened up fire with the 50-caliber machine gun that was mounted on the APC in order to give our vehicle some cover from the incoming fire. My APC then spun around, the tailgate lowered and Lt. Humphrey, SP4 Van Eck and PFC Perez ran out of the APC and toward the wounded commander. I continued to provide cover with the 50-caliber machine gun. SP4 Van Eck and PFC Perez took position a few feet away from the wounded commander and continued to fire into the thick bush. I witnessed Lt. Humphrey and SP4 Van Eck at one point helping the wounded commander prepare to be placed into our APC. The gunfire was so heavy and loud at this point that you could not hear another person speak.

"During the rescue, someone had called in friendly fire support from a U.S. Army Huey helicopter. Unfortunately, as the Huey opened fire in our direction, one of the Engineers was wounded in the back of the leg. He was positioned close to our APC. I continued to man the 50-celiber as my APC began to take four of the seriously wounded Engineers back to the nearby aid station. In the confusion, I noticed that SP4 Van Eck and PFC Perez were left behind as we drove away. I could do nothing about this because the driver made the decision to pull out and I was still in the back of the APC, manning the machine gun.

"When I got back to the Aid Station, I realized that my canteen, web belt, and ammo pouch all had bullet holes in them. Those in my APC took the lead in saving the lives of many Engineers that day.

"The reason there were so many Viet Cong in the area (approximately 4,000) is because we later found out that their underground headquarters were located in this area. I found the bravery of SP4 Van Eck and PFC Perez extraordinary given their young age and the fact that they volunteered to what turned out to be the spearhead of an extremely dangerous rescue attempt of an officer not even in their unit. They voluntarily risked their lives to save the lives of those they did not even know." – Signed, MSGT. Orvie J. Gosnell (Retired).

Gosnell, who would retire from the Army in 1969 after 21 years of service, was an early leader in 2/32 after the battalion arrived in RVN on Nov. 3, 1965. He had already served one tour of duty in Vietnam and knew the area around Saigon quite well.

"Since I had been there once, I believe I was useful," Gosnell admitted in his letter. "I knew my way around Saigon. We were set up just outside Saigon towards Bien Hoa, near the University of Saigon. It was real nice going back because I seemed to know half the people in Saigon, former employees and the like. I had worked in the club system on my first tour. I ran General Stillwell's mess tent right outside the main gate of Tan Son Nhut Base. I met a lot of important people on my first tour. But you couldn't trust the Chinese in the Cholon District (of Saigon). They would steal anything they could get their hands on!"

Gosnell ran a very efficient mess tent for Charlie Company until his transfer orders came through. Bill Van Eck was still raving about his cooking 53 years later.

"There wasn't anything he couldn't make tasty for us soldiers," Van Eck admitted.

Van Eck and Gosnell developed a friendship that lasted until JD passed away at his Arkansas home in 2015.

"JD was an infantryman in the Korean War," Van Eck said in February 2019. "Most of his company were either killed or wounded and he was injured, too. Later on in his life, those old wounds caught up with JD, confining him to a wheelchair and then he was bedridden (before he died). I was able to help get him a wheelchair through a friend of mine who was head of the DAV's women's auxiliary, a lady named Linda Turrelo. She put pressure on the VA. JD and I talked by phone a lot in his later years. We spoke of our old unit, the Proud Americans, including our battalion commander, Col. Leon DeCorrevent."

Through battalion reunions that began in 1999, Van Eck was able to learn more about JD Gosnell.

"JD retired as a Master Sergeant. But I remember him as one great Proud American. When our battalion arrived in Vietnam, JD was already there. He was with the advance party. This was his second tour of Vietnam. He had a hot meal waiting for us, with his famous biscuits. All of the other batteries were eating C-rations out of a can. We were lucky to have JD in C Battery during our first few months in Vietnam."

Without Korean War veteran JD Gosnell manning the machine gun on that rescue mission in Trung Lap, things might have turned out a lot worse for the soldiers in Charlie Company, First Engineers.

LION IN WINTER – Wardell Hollis and wife Brenda retired to his hometown of San Antonio. (Photo courtesy of Wardell Hollis)

CHAPTER FIFTEEN
Wardell Hollis Followed His Mother's Advice

BY WARDELL HOLLIS

Growing up in San Antonio, I was raised by working parents, lived in a Christian home, and initially attended public segregated schools which included Grant Elementary School, Dorie Miller Elementary School, and Douglas Junior High School. My introduction to sports came in junior high school when I began playing football and basketball.

San Antonio schools were integrated in 1955 at the start of my teenage years. The integration process went smoothly because of the city's diverse ethnic population. Black students could attend any integrated school as long as they could get transportation to their chosen school. We used public transportation to get to school. Upon graduating from Douglas Junior High, I enrolled at Brackenridge High School.

My football coach, Weldon Forren, switched me to end, a position that I loved to play. He saw something special in me and mentored me as an athlete and person during my high school days.

I enjoyed participating in the high school ROTC program because it taught leadership and rifle marksmanship skills. Additionally, wearing the ROTC uniform distinguished cadets from other high school students. Like other cadets, I took pride in wearing the ROTC uniform, learning to shoot a weapon, and becoming a member of the Brackenridge High School Drill Team. We marched in the San Antonio parades and participated in local high school competitions.

While playing center on the basketball team during my junior school year, we won the city conference championship for the 1959-60 season. I also ran hurdles on the track team primarily to stay in shape and improve my speed and agility.

During my senior year, Coach Forren decided to convert me to fullback as I was one of the bigger players on the team. This change of position and my performance during my senior year resulted in me being selected to the "All-City Football Team." I also earned the "Thom McAn Shoe Award" as the city's best all-around football player. Because of this award, along with Coach Forren's influence and impact on my life, I was offered numerous college football scholarships including several from Big Eight conference schools. My combination of size (6-foot-3, 193 pounds) and speed drew the attention of many college football coaches. I even considered attending West Point to play football.

A General officer at Fort Sam Houston introduced me to the idea of going to West Point. He sent me some yearbooks. I looked them over and didn't see pictures of female cadets. The General explained that females were not allowed to attend the United States Military Academy at West Point. That was the basis for me deciding not to go to West Point. In retrospect, I wish someone knowledgeable could have informed me about the significance of a West Point education and how that relates to an Army career. Having a different perspective on West Point could have altered my decision to attend.

My high school counselor arranged for me to take the College Entrance Examination. The results indicated I was border-line in one area. When I asked the counselor for advice, she advised me to attend a vocational school instead of college.

The thought of not attending college was very disappointing. I told my mother what the counselor had said. I still remember what she told me: "Never let someone decide what you can or cannot do in life. If you believe that you can do something and are willing to put forth the effort, you can do anything."

I followed my mother's advice and decided to review my football scholarship offers one more time.

Football recruiters from Oklahoma State showed a lot of interest in me and I soon accepted their scholarship offer. In September 1961, I enrolled at the campus in Stillwater where I would spend the next four years of my life. As a freshman, I achieved a 2.7 grade point average. I was proud of this accomplishment and looked forward to seeing how pleased my mother would be.

A day after completing my last examination, the head football coach called me into his office and said my father had called and needed me to come home immediately because my mother was seriously ill. That was all I knew. I tried to reach my father, to no avail.

I had a strong sense that my mother was in a life-threatening situation. I was put on a plane and flown to San Antonio where I was able to visit with my mother for approximately seven hours before she died of leukemia. She had been battling this disease for several years but both my mother and father did not want me to know, for fear I would not attend college if I knew she was sick.

My mother's death was devastating to me. I almost quit college. Concentrating on my studies was extremely difficult. Eventually, I recalled my mother's desire for me to graduate from college and this memory got me back on the right path.

I played a lot on offense during my sophomore season. (Editor's note: Records indicate Hollis carried the ball 69 times for 331 yards, an average of 4.8 yards per carry. He also caught 12 passes for 95 yards.) My best memory was beating West Point. The New York newspaper headlines before we played them said something like '"Oklahoma Who?" because we were always overshadowed by the University of Oklahoma. But we beat Army, which meant a lot to me because I almost went there.

Oklahoma State hired a new football coach in my junior year. This coach was a former Alabama assistant. To get our attention, the new coach ran us through a demanding spring training football camp that was similar to scenes in the movie, "The Junction Boys." (A movie that depicted Bear Bryant's torturous training camp at Texas A&M in 1954.) Scholarship football players were quitting so fast that at the beginning of the season, Oklahoma State had just over two teams of players available to suit up for games. I personally had gone from 224 in spring practice to 179 pounds at the beginning of the season.

I played mostly on the defensive side during my final two varsity seasons. Football paved my way to a college degree but my future was really locked up in ROTC.

In the 1960s, many colleges made ROTC mandatory for all male students in the first two years of college. After two years of ROTC, you had to make a decision to drop out or apply for the Advanced ROTC program. It was kind of unusual for a football player to take the advanced program but I wanted to become a regular Army officer.

During those final two years of Advanced ROTC, I became friends with a fellow student, Oklahoma native Gary Perryman, who also had firm plans to become a career Army officer. I met Gary in my junior year. He befriended me. We talked a lot about our potential careers in the Army. We pledged the Scabbard and Blade ROTC fraternity together. Gary would sometimes invite me to eat with him at his fraternity house. Years later, Gary let me know that some of his fraternity brothers were not on board with me eating dinner there. In general, students and staff were nice to minority students, but there was very little social co-mingling between black and white students. Black students found entertainment by dancing in the OSU Student Union, or attending parties at the Alpha Phi Alpha black fraternity house or at someone's apartment, playing cards.

I did meet my future wife, Brenda, in college, a union that continues more than 50 years later through various Army postings and my final assignment at The Pentagon before I retired in 2004.

I graduated from Oklahoma State in 1966. Normally, an ROTC cadet would attend "Summer Camp" between his junior and senior year. However, I had to work during the summer of my junior year, which required me to attend ROTC summer camp after I graduated from Oklahoma State University. So, after completing summer camp at Fort Sill, I was commissioned as a Second Lieutenant in the U.S. Army. I still remember the day I was commissioned as an officer in the Army -- July 26, 1966. My first assignment took me to Fort Carson, Colorado. Because of my date of rank, I became the battery's Executive Officer for the first two commanders I served with. Each of them was sent to Vietnam. After the second one left, I was installed as battery commander and promoted to First Lieutenant. Later on, I earned my promotion to Captain.

In the summer of 1968, I got my orders to Vietnam. While waiting to leave, Brenda delivered our first child on August 18, 1968. We named her Pamela. I left for Vietnam on September 17, 1968, my second wedding anniversary. Upon arriving in Vietnam, who did I see first? Gary Perryman. Now I should tell you, Gary and I had not communicated with each other since attending the Field Artillery Basic Course at Fort Sill, Oklahoma three years earlier. He left Fort Sill for an assignment in Alaska and I went to Fort Carson. We were both so busy; we could not keep in touch. When I reached Vietnam, the Army assigned me to the 23rd Artillery Group in Phu Loi. As I walked into headquarters, one of the first people I saw was Gary Perryman. It was great seeing him again.

Gary had been in Vietnam for three months and had a good feel for what was going on in the 23rd Group. Gary said 23rd Artillery Group was considering sending me to command A Battery in the 2/32 battalion. He said he didn't think it was a good fit for me because they had some "issues" in that unit. I didn't know what he meant at the time. Because the A Battery commander had been severely wounded on Sept. 17, Group Headquarters assigned me to replace him.

My new unit had been under siege at Camp Saint Barbara (aka French Fort) six miles north of Tay Ninh City. The only road to the base had been shut down in early September after seven soldiers were killed by land mines in a period of two months' time. A Battery had been mortared every day from Aug. 6 to Sept. 17, when a mortar round took off the legs of Battery Commander Don Babb and killed two infantry officers standing with him. A medevac helicopter rushed Babb back to Cu Chi Base Camp for surgery.

Once I got my orders, I boarded a chopper and flew into the besieged Camp Saint Barbara. It was a small chopper and the pilot kept making these hard descents in and then pulling up at the last moment. We would come in, back off, circle and come in again. Finally, we made a hard landing. I reached over to shake the pilot's hand. He pushed my hand away, threw my duffel bag out of the chopper and pushed me out.

That's how dangerous it was at French Fort. The chopper pilots wanted no part of it.

My first impressions of Camp Saint Barbara? Well, when you are replacing someone who has been medically evacuated, your first priority is to ensure that we were able to defend ourselves against an attack. I had to make certain our soldiers could carry out their mission of providing fire support. One thing I learned right away was the enemy could observe our routines from a distant mountain. We had to change our daily schedule for doing things, like when we ate, or showered. We scheduled "Mad Minutes" (unannounced weapons firing) at different times during the night, just to keep the enemy guessing. Sometimes, attacks occurred when the enemy believed that soldiers were asleep.

The camp defense seemed secure. We had four Quad 50s (four 50-caliber machine guns mounted on the back of a 2 ½ ton truck, one in each corner of the fire base). The berm stood five or six feet tall. It was surrounded by barbed wire and had fighting positions and claymore mines built into it. There was one road leading into the camp and when it was not in use, we had a truck blocking the entrance.

It didn't take long to figure out what the "issues" were that my friend Gary Perryman worried about back at 23rd Group headquarters. Gary's concern was that part of the defense equation involved having an "attached unit" working with us. This unit served to reinforce our overall camp defense. Gary felt like there should be somebody senior to a captain in command of the fire base, someone who could have authority over the attached unit (Quad 50s and their men).

The enemy seemed to have backed off a bit after its Sept. 17 mortar barrage that disabled Captain Babb and killed two officers standing next to him. We were still getting mortared but no attacks. There were definitely probes of our defenses at night. We would see trip flares going off in the darkness. Sometimes dead bodies were observed in the outer perimeter the next morning. Changing our routines was critical to our survival.

Two of our soldiers were killed in this stretch, one in an accident involving a firearm, and another while burning gunpowder outside the berm. Strange things could happen in a combat fire base. A job at the end of each day was to burn the excess powder that had gone unused. A soldier was performing this task when a helicopter came in to deliver items and wanted to land. We warned the pilot to back off but he hovered above the powder. His chopper blades spread the fire faster than expected. The soldier could not escape that fire and received fatal burns to his body. His death was a terrible tragedy.

I found my artillery soldiers to be great in providing fire support to units who were within our firing range. I was only there 90 days before they transferred me to the 2/27 Artillery Battalion. Looking back on my stay with the 2/32, I was not impressed by the support from our battalion commander. He was more concerned with how our soldiers looked than how well they did their jobs. Did they have clean uniforms and shined boots? I wanted my soldiers to focus on equipment maintenance, fighting positions, and understanding their jobs during an attack. Those were my priorities.

After three months, I was sent to command another field artillery battery that was located near Long Binh, not far from Saigon. I would serve out the rest of my tour with 2/27, 155 self-propelled battalion.

I look back on my tour and feel great about my duty in Vietnam. Soldiers were protected and kept alive.

I took my Freedom Bird flight home in August 1969, arriving at Travis Air Force Base near San Francisco, which was the heart of the anti-war movement. We were not received well by the protestors. And my trip was interesting for a different reason. While waiting for my flight from Oakland to Oklahoma City, an ambulance came into the airport to pick up a couple of people and when it left, they turned the siren on, not far from me. I reacted the way I always did to sirens in Vietnam that signaled incoming mortar or rockets. I hit the ground. People in the airport looked at me like I was a drunk. I got up, dusted myself off, and hid myself from the public until it was time to board my plane.

Still only 25 years old, I had to do some thinking and planning for the future of myself and my family. I thought about getting out of the Army but then I realized maybe the Army would pay for me getting a Master's degree while still in uniform. The Army would not send me to school to get a Master's degree, but God opened up another door and it worked out. I was assigned to be an ROTC instructor at Prairie View A&M University which created an avenue for me to work on getting a

Master's degree. I taught ROTC classes and completed my requirements for a Master's in Guidance Counseling.

In 1978, the Army sent me to Germany and I commanded my third Field Artillery battery. It was a great experience and I learned a lot. I left Germany and went to Fort Leavenworth, to attend the Command and General Staff College. While there, I was promoted to Major. My next assignment was to the Training and Doctrine Command at Fort Monroe. When I finished that tour, I was promoted to Lt. Colonel.

After that, the Army sent me to be an Instructor at the Armed Forces Staff College. Some of my students went on to become General Officers in the military.

The next assignment was to South Korea. I spent a year there as a Joint Staff Officer and then completed the War College course.

The next stop put me at the Pentagon where I worked in the Deputy Chief of Staff's Personnel Office. When passed over for Colonel, I decided to retire, having served 22 years and 7 months in the Army.

While working in the Pentagon, I decided I wanted to do something different with my life. After I retired from the Army, I applied for a job with the Washington D.C. school district. The school system created an Inspector General Office and I was the first person to serve as the District of Columbia's Public Inspector General. I did this job for three years, until it started to feel like I was doing Army work again. I had always wanted to work with children when I retired. I became a school counselor, then an assistant principal and finally an elementary school principal, all in the District of Columbia public schools.

I retired in 2004 and moved back to San Antonio with Brenda in 2007. In retirement, I have had time to reflect on my life. I notice some changes as I grow older. When I was in the Army, I put my total faith in the leadership of our nation. When I was in Vietnam, the Commander In Chief, our President, gave the orders and I never questioned them. I thought the demonstrators were un-American. I was kind of negative about the people who were against the war. But as I grew older, and did some reading, let's just say my position has changed. I am older and wiser. I now see Vietnam and other wars with more wisdom. As a retired soldier, I can question why we use United States' military power. I question why we go to war.

I guess now I am a *Lion in Winter*, living back in my hometown, reaping the rewards of a life well-lived. I have seen the world and come back home again to San Antonio. Full circle, back to the place where I grew up. The world has changed a lot and so have I.

KEEPING BUSY – Captain Gary Perryman, right, poses with First Sergeant Young at Tay Ninh Base Camp during the autumn of 1968. (Photo courtesy of Gary Perryman)

CHAPTER SIXTEEN
GARY PERRYMAN SUMS UP
HIS EXPERIENCES

BY TERRY NAU

Gary Perryman is the sum of all his experiences. And now, in his late 70s, this old soldier looks back on a life that began on the dusty plains of Oklahoma, continued at Oklahoma State University, expanded during an Army assignment in Alaska and then reached a new level of adrenalin when the Vietnam War pulled him into the most compelling experience of his youthful existence.

Like many Vietnam War veterans, Gary Perryman grew up fast.

"I have always thought if I wrote an autobiography, the title would be 'Emperor of Arapaho,' " Perryman admitted early in 2019. "My family originally lived in Arapaho, Oklahoma where my father, Grady Perryman, headed a small automobile loan department for the local bank. Arapaho was the county seat of Custer County. I was born on Easter Sunday in 1941. I had an older sister by six years. My birth was a big day for my parents. They wanted me to become a doctor but I blew that out of the water by age seven.

"By the time I turned 18 months old, I started finding my way around this small, dusty town on the central prairie of Oklahoma. I would visit various stores and get things I wanted, like a haircut, ice cream at the drug store, or candy at the gas station, and the owners would collect from my father when they saw him. I truly was the 'Emperor of Arapaho.' Until my father died in March 1943. At the age of 29, he died from an undiagnosed congenital kidney disease. My mother was 25 and a widow with three young children. She remarried seven months later. My new stepfather was a minister. We moved to Albuquerque where he became minister of a rescue mission."

Perryman's family would subsequently move to Portland, Oregon for a spell before his mother engineered a final move back home to Oklahoma, just outside Tulsa, where her son finally put down some roots. Gary joined the National Guard in 1958. After he graduated from high school in 1959, Perryman took his basic training at Fort Leonard Wood, Mo. His early instruction came in the infantry before he returned to civilian life, with the National Guard duty taking away two weeks of his summers for the next six years.

"I took a job rebuilding a sewage treatment plant in Seminole, OK," Perryman recalled, thinking back to his first adult working experience. "One day in the winter of 1959-60, I was on a jackhammer, breaking cement in the freezing rain. I thought to myself, 'In 10 years, I might become a foreman. Ten years after that, I might be a job site superintendent.' No matter what, I was still going to be working outdoors in the freezing rain."

Having looked into the future, Perryman changed the course of his life and decided to attend college. He enrolled at Oklahoma State University with the goal of becoming a physics major. This self-made young man joined the required ROTC program, graduated in 1965 with a degree in physics, and shortly thereafter went on active duty with the Army.

"Most people don't remember that ROTC was mandatory back in my day," Perryman wrote in an exchange of emails with the author in December 2018. "In the early 1960s, our corps of mandatory ROTC was around 4,500 people. Today it is more like 100-300. I was already in the Oklahoma National Guard so I was able to compress my ROTC training into one year. The junior and senior courses were taken simultaneously and summer camp followed. I had broken up with my girlfriend of three years. I was a sergeant with the Guard and had one more year left of college. The Army was short of infantry NCOs in the active force and was taking reserve people to fill the ranks. I probably would have gone to Vietnam as a buck sergeant. There was no way I wanted to go to war that way.

"I went to the ROTC in college and they showed me the red carpet. That's where I first met Wardell Hollis. He was a tailback and defensive back on the Oklahoma State football team. Walt Garrison (future Dallas Cowboys star) was the fullback. On a training mission for ROTC, we hit an ambush. I was the platoon leader. As I gathered people to move out of the area, I noticed someone in a hole was not moving to join the unit. Reaching into the hole, I grabbed the person's collar and started pulling. As I pulled, the person just kept getting bigger and bigger. I figured I had better keep pulling as someone this big (6-3, 200 pounds) needed to be held tight. That was Wardell. We became friends and later met at the 23rd Field Artillery Group Headquarters in Phu Loi, Republic of Vietnam.

"ROTC 'force-branched' me into the artillery because they were in need of Lieutenants and I had already passed the math exam, so it was field artillery for me. This was the best thing that could have happened. I loved the artillery. The soldiers were much sharper than found in the infantry. The FDC soldiers were great mentally, in most cases. The NCOs were very sharp and knowledgeable in their specialties. And the only limits were the imagination of the artillery soldier."

Perryman's new career in the Army first took him to Alaska, where he picked up valuable experience working with artillery units that featured small guns (105mm) and the medium-sized (155mm). Gary started out as a forward observer. He trained in every officer position before becoming battery commander of a medium gun unit. His skill set would serve him well in Southeast Asia, where over 500,000 American troops were now serving in the war zone.

By the time Captain Perryman reached the Republic of Vietnam in June 1968, his experience working with artillery batteries as well as a special assignment with higher headquarters set him apart from the more inexperienced officers coming into the war zone.

"I was assigned to 23rd Artillery Group headquarters at Phu Loi for my first few months," Perryman recalled. "It was an interesting job because we saw all the top operations, to include intelligence reports for western II Corps. This allowed better decisions in operations for our fighting units. As an example, one of our batteries was firing a contact mission to the south of Tay Ninh. I was monitoring the radio net when an FDC soldier stated they had heard a voice with an Australian accent saying, 'Check fire. You are bloody killing us.' I told the Fire Direction Officer to keep firing because the only Aussies we knew about were 70 miles away. This voice they heard was an imposter. The North Vietnamese Army trained people in linguistics and they would use fake accents over our radio networks and telephone lines. We kept firing that mission and nobody ever complained.

"Another time, I spoke to the enemy on our phone line at group. This person identified himself as a Lieutenant in the 2nd Battalion, 32nd Field Artillery. He said he was calling in the morning ammunition report. I started to write down the numbers. Something in his report seemed wrong. After the phone conversation ended, I went to the ammo report file and noted the numbers I had been given were the same as the ammo report from the week before. That never happens. About an hour later, the real Lieutenant phoned in his report. So you can see how devious the enemy really was. By this point in the war, we were dealing mainly with the North Vietnamese Army (NVA) in the western III Field Force region known as War Zones C and D."

Perryman recalled how the 25th Infantry Division captured a NVA signal unit in an area near Go Dau Ha village, located a few clicks from Cu Chi base camp, a major American outpost around 40 miles northwest of Saigon.

"There were a few well-trained linguists among the prisoners," Perryman said. "They could handle multiple accents very well. That was where the Aussie voice I heard had come from."

To eliminate this communications trickery by the enemy, the 23rd Group Signal Corps detachment established a radio relay on top of Nui Ba Den Mountain. Needing to have another way of communicating with the group battalions, this relay solved the problem of enemy interference.

Captain Perryman received orders to take over B Battery in October 1968. He would remain as battery commander until returning home in June 1969. His experience with smaller artillery units in Alaska proved useful right away.

"I was eating lunch one day when an order came down for a platoon of 8-inch to move east near a rubber plantation for a couple days. My XO was at the table with me, finishing up his meal. I told him to get the platoon ready while I finished my meal. Going over to the firing battery, the platoon was ready to move and I reported ready to move to the battalion. A call came back that the battalion XO was on his way over to inspect the group. Having a background with light and medium units, moving was nothing (difficult) for me."

Nevertheless, the move did run into an obstacle.

"A problem in movement was caused by higher headquarters directing heavy units to place all ammo in bunkers," Perryman said. "That is not the best idea in combat. We placed ammo in bunkers, but we kept two five-ton trucks loaded with ammo in ditches, in a safer area. We could bulldoze a trench the size of the truck and back the loaded trucks into the ditch. Sand bags were placed around the engine to keep fragments from damaging this area. The sides of the ditch protected the tires. This process allowed us to always be able to move in a timely manner. The battalion XO came over and checked the column. He found it as was instructed. In later moves, he would come out to inspect but let us get on the road with minimal delay."

Because of this efficiency in movement, B Battery was assigned many of these platoon missions over the time Perryman commanded this unit.

Looking back on his time in Vietnam, Perryman is reminded of the inexperience he saw among many young officers.

"Before I went to Vietnam, I was helped by being a battery commander in Alaska," he said. "In Nam, we were very short on that kind of experience among our officers. That was why the battalion commander used Majors to command two of the batteries. When my tour ended, I was replaced by Wade Rishel, a very seasoned Captain from West Point. I was very proud of the work the firing battery people did during my nine months with B Battery. We had a great unit in spite of limits to training and experience. Most of the FDC guys had college degrees, or spent time in higher education. Our gun sections worked hard and improved and were very effective under the guidance of Lt. Zavaledreiga, or Lt. Z, as we called him. He worked well with our chief of firing battery, SFC Riddle."

Gary Perryman, now living in Salt Lake City, looks back on his time in a war zone with the curiosity and attention to detail that marked his career as a combat officer.

"We all remember events from our time in Vietnam that happened close to us," he said. "I can remember the names of the battery commanders who preceded and followed me with B Battery – Neil Springborn and Wade Rishel. I will never forget my one Christmas in Vietnam, with B Battery at Tay Ninh base camp. The troops placed a small branch of a tree in the sandbags by the front door of the hooch that the First Sergeant and I used. They hung C-Ration lids and trinkets as decorations on the tree. Top Sergeant and I were inside, dining on a care package my college professor uncle had sent. My uncle had been a Marine in Korea and understood how goodies from home were welcomed. Dr. John T. Hubbell was a buck sergeant in the Marine Artillery back in the 1950s. He was most considerate. I also remember around Christmas, a noise erupted outside our hooch. It was the troops. And Lt. Noble. They were singing carols. Even today, I often have lunch with Major Keith Painter, who was our battalion XO. He lives not far from me in Bountiful, Utah. Keith is a retired Colonel who enjoys restoring old cars."

Perryman values those friendships he made in Vietnam. Like many Vietnam War veterans, he also reflects back on those complicated days of his youth.

"I think about the racial tension in Vietnam," Perryman added. "Growing up in Oklahoma, I worked in the fields with blacks and learned early on to watch for things that might get out of control. I tried to prevent bad stuff from happening. Going through infantry training, I saw what racial difficulties can do to a military unit. I wanted to create an environment to prevent bad stuff from happening. My friendship with Wardell Hollis in college was helpful. He sometimes visited the fraternity house where I lived. Not all of the people in the house were friendly to blacks. But we never had an incident.

"I remember in Vietnam when the A Battery commander was almost fragged. Two of the soldiers suspected of causing trouble were sent to B Battery. One of them just pushed past me one day. I stopped him and said there was no need to salute an officer but there should be a greeting. My top sergeant just laughed when he saw this. As I entered the Orderly Room, he said, 'You just met one of our new people from A Battery.'

"A few weeks later, the same soldier refused to pick up some trash and ended up in my office. I started an Article 15 on him as I never allowed a soldier to disobey orders from an NCO. The soldier refused the punishment and said he wanted a summary court martial. The summary officer was a black, Major Horton, who ran Service Battery. He came over to do the summary court and I gave him my desk. Then I went to the mess for a cup of coffee. As I finished filling my cup, I heard the screen door open and close. It was Major Horton. He went over to the coffee and poured himself a cup. Then he came to my table. Looking at me, he said, 'You can go over and give the Article 15 now.' Horton said the soldier started talking black jargon to him. Horton told him he was not his 'bro,' and if he thought he was going to get off better in a summary court with a black officer, he had another think coming. That soldier was soon busted down to E2 but then he started soldiering and doing well.

"This same soldier came to me and asked for an extension to stay longer in Vietnam but I refused. I thought he should go home and think about things before coming back to RVN. Then I noticed a tear on his face. I told him how I had busted him as low as I could and made life miserable for him. His response to me was, 'Yes sir, you did, but you always treated me like a man.' "

Perryman treated all of his soldiers like men, asking only that they do their jobs in return.

"I was threatened a few times," he recalled. "A white soldier threatened to shoot me at Duc Lap once. The next night, there were VC in the village nearby. They killed the village chief because he had talked to us. Laying in the grass outside that village, listening, I whispered for this same soldier to come up with the M-60. He crawled up beside me. In the dark, I could still see his hands were shaking. I said, 'Yesterday, you were going to shoot me. I hope you will shoot tonight if needed.' The VC disappeared into the night and the sun came up the next morning."

Those memories of the war sometimes return to this old soldier in his retirement. But Gary Perryman is quick to brush them aside, preferring to talk about his amazing wife and children. It was his wife, Cathy, who stood by him when the family curse – congenital kidney failure – struck Gary in the 1970s.

"Doctors told me I probably had one year to live," he recalled. "I had to take a medical retirement from the Army in 1976 so that my family could receive survivor's benefits. At that time, the benefits were not given to soldiers on active duty. I had spent seven years in the National Guard and 11 years on active duty in the Army before I retired."

Fortunately, Perryman's congenital kidney failure was brought under control, thanks to research breakthroughs at the University of Utah. The retired soldier went to work for seven years in industry before taking a high school teaching assignment in physics. Perryman finished up his working career as an educator, also filling in as a part-time football coach.

"I must tell you about my family," Perryman said. "My wife, Catherine Mary Tucci, had a most distinguished career as a teacher and principal. As a girl, Cathy spent five years at a girls' school in Naples, Italy. She spoke fluent Italian, as well as French, German and even some Japanese. She earned her Master's degree from Columbia University in New York City. We were married in 1966. Our son, Theodore Max Perryman, graduated from West Point. He has two sons. Our daughter Julie graduated from George Washington University and works as a lobbyist. She has four children."

Sadly, Cathy Perryman passed away in 2013. Gary bides his time in retirement, visiting his children and grandchildren, looking back over a life filled with all kinds of experiences. His father died young from an undiagnosed kidney ailment and Gary almost suffered the same fate. He worked in construction for a year before realizing that college might be a better option for his skill set. Amazingly, Gary Perryman became a physics major in college, an Army officer, a husband, father and grandfather. Truly, he is the sum of all his experiences.

WHERE'S THE FORT? – Dick Muth and wife Darlene stand with Vietnamese farmer Say on their return trip to a fire support base Muth helped build in 1967. Over 40 years, nature had returned the fort almost to its original form. (Photo courtesy of Dick Muth)

CHAPTER SEVENTEEN
Return to Vietnam

BY TERRY NAU

Dick Muth is one of many Vietnam War veterans who entertained thoughts of returning to the place that held so many of his memories from over 50 years ago.

"Vietnam was never far from my mind," Muth said in March 2019. This is a man who completed his stint in the war and went back home to South Dakota in 1968, eventually building his own electrical company, enabling a lifestyle that allowed Dick and his wife Darlene to visit 46 different countries over the ensuing years.

But there was always one country that Dick wanted to see again.

"I started thinking about returning to Vietnam when 40 years had passed," Muth admitted. "And then in the summer of 2017, I was on a long car ride, playing 60s music. You always remember those songs that we heard in Vietnam. I realized 50 years was coming up. It was time to go back. A Vietnam veteran from my hometown had been back twice and he told me we really ought to do it. After talking to him, I went back to Darlene and tried to convince her to come with me. Darlene was hesitant at first but then she agreed."

The January 2018 trip became very personal for Muth, who would make friends with his Vietnamese guide and a farmer who led the former Army engineer back to a location called "French Fort" that had been the last place where Muth worked before leaving country 50 years earlier.

"That area did not even have a name, as far as I knew," Muth said. "For some reason, this was the place I wanted to see most of all. I did not want to go on a group tour and have to go to places the other guys wanted to see. I had a list of about six places where I had been that were distinct in my mind. Vung Tau beach – where I arrived by ship in 1967 after 23 days at sea. The base camps at Tay Ninh and Cu Chi. The port of Newport, north of Saigon, where we unloaded a lot of equipment. Two air bases – Long Binh and Bien Hoa. But most of all, I wanted to see that base we were helping to build in my last two months in Vietnam."

A little background on this plot of land might help. After establishing major Army base camps in Cu Chi and Tay Ninh in 1967, the II Field Force command center began focusing on building smaller artillery fire support bases across Tay Ninh Province northwest of Saigon, close to the Cambodia border. Intersecting lines of fire from the heavy guns of several battalions would provide support for infantry troops and harass both the Viet Cong and North Vietnamese Army troops who roamed through the region.

In the autumn of 1967, engineers started bulldozing dirt for a base that the Army would name Camp Saint Barbara. Originally a holdover from the French army's ill-fated occupation, the more commonly known "French Fort" was located approximately seven miles north of Nui Ba Den Mountain. The mountain served as a landmark for this province, an ominous 3,300-foot tall fortress that rose above the flatlands and marshy rice paddies. An American Signal Corps company worked uneasily on top of the mountain, functioning as a vital relay station for military radio networks. The enemy controlled the area below, almost down to ground level. American soldiers liked to call the place "Black Virgin Mountain." Vietnamese preferred the tamer "Black Lady Mountain." No matter the name, this was a scary place.

A dirt road from Tay Ninh wound around the base of the mountain. Once Camp Saint Barbara began taking shape, American trucks would become a familiar site on this trail, and Viet Cong soldiers often dug mines into the road overnight, hoping to blow up a truck or personnel carrier.

In time, the road became so dangerous that 10 American soldiers died in separate land mine incidents between June and early September 1968, resulting in the closure of the only ground access into Camp Saint Barbara.

"I remember when we first started going out there," said Muth, a truck driver for the 43rd Engineer Company. "The minesweepers would go over the road first and then we would drive out behind them later in the morning. I recall one of our trucks did hit a mine. We started working at the site in mid-November 1967. The bulldozers had already pushed up three sides of the berm and were working on the north berm when we arrived. We had our Thanksgiving meal out there. We worked all day, hauling laterite (dirt) in our dump trucks, from the east side of the camp, into the camp for the engineers to use. At night, we slept next to the berm in our sleeping bags. I had already been in country for 10 months and was due to go home in January. So this was my last duty in Vietnam.

"I found out much later that the site was originally called French Fort," Muth added. "I went home and got married, raised a family, started my own company, but I never really forgot about Vietnam. I would wonder what happened to that camp we built over my final two months in Vietnam. It never really left my mind. I would try to find it on Google Earth but my memory was really just that the camp was about five to eight miles north of the mountain. After Darlene and I decided to make the trip back to Vietnam, I found a guy in Philadelphia who could arrange individual tours. He hired me a guide that we met at the airport in Ho Chi Minh City."

After visiting 46 countries over the years, Dick and Darlene Muth were experienced world travelers, and well prepared for this exhausting journey.

"Darlene and I normally fly in coach but I wanted to fly first class back to Vietnam," Muth said. "I had spent 23 days on a boat coming over to Vietnam the first time. And this was a long flight. We're a lot older. We booked first class and it was great. The guide met us at the airport and we talked about our trip, what we would do the next day. The place I really wanted to see was that old fire base. Our guide took us up past the mountain and we started looking around but it was hard to find anything. Fortunately, the place we stayed at that night had Wi-Fi. I got on the Internet and googled 'French Fort' and came up with a guy from my old unit who had the GPS data for French Fort. The guide took us to that area and we pulled into a farmer's yard. I was not convinced this was the place. The farmer's name was Say. I started asking him questions about French Fort with our translator in the middle, helping us along. Say told me he remembered the old fort. Say was around 12 years old when the camp was operating. I asked him where the helicopters landed and he said they landed outside the berm. That was correct. He remembered us hauling all the dirt into the site. I asked him where did we find the dirt and he showed me, on

219

the east side of the road. Say said the locals used that site as a garbage dump until about 20 years ago.

"Say remembered when the jet planes came in and dropped napalm outside the fort. He made noises to simulate the sound of the flames hitting the ground. As were walking, I realized we were near the old west berm, where a Twin-40 gun had been situated 50 years ago. Those things made a lot of noise! I asked Say if he remembered and he got real excited and started to go ... boom ... boom. I knew for sure that he had been there.

"It was getting late. We decided to meet the next day. That next morning, Say took us to the big hole where we dug out the laterite. It was all grown over. The old base was mostly jungle. But when I asked Say about the front gate, he said it's still there. We drove over to the front gate. It's a new gate, really, built by the Vietnamese. Turns out, part of the old base is a Vietnamese training camp. The guard wouldn't let us go in. What we found out is the old French Fort is part training camp and the rest is jungle.

"We walked around some more. I am pretty certain we found the area where I used to sleep next to the berm," Muth continued. "This was pretty emotional for me. I was glad Darlene was there."

Maybe because Darlene was there, the Muths struck up a real friendship with the farmer Say and his family.

"Never in my wildest dreams as a soldier did I think I would return to Vietnam and become friends with a Vietnamese farmer and his family," Muth admitted. "We spent a few hours with Say on the first day but it gets dark around 5 o'clock in Vietnam during January. We asked if we could come back again the next morning and Say agreed. Say and his wife had identical twin grandsons, around eight years old. They were born three weeks after our own identical twin grandsons were born back home. So when we returned to Tay Ninh that night, we went shopping for gifts. We bought toy trucks and a few other small gifts and took them with us in the morning. The kids were thrilled. Say had a very nice house, around 10 years old, with a porch in the back where we sat and drank tea and talked."

Even with a language barrier, the two men managed to communicate.

"I asked Say if he had ever seen an American dollar bill and he said he hadn't. I reached in my wallet and pulled out a ten dollar bill and gave it to him as a gift. Say said he would frame it and hang it in his living room."

There was some sadness that Say related to the Muths during their visit.

"The old minefield next to the fort killed between nine and eleven farmers after the war ended," Muth said. "Say said the last explosion occurred in 1992. One farmer died when his water buffalo wandered into the minefield and he chased after him."

Say's neighborhood also felt the effects of Agent Orange and napalm that were delivered by American aircraft during the war.

"I asked Say about the napalm and told him I was sorry. I became a little tearful and Say said don't worry about it and gave me a hug. He said the Vietnamese only look to the future, not the past."

Say's parents were loyal to the South Vietnamese government, which might explain his willingness to forgive the Americans who visited his home.

"Say told us there were a lot of tunnels in the area and the Viet Cong planned to use them at some point," Muth said. "I never knew they had tunnels around there."

Muth also asked Say if the Americans had left anything valuable behind when they abandoned Camp Saint Barbara.

"He laughed and said, 'Not much, mostly junk.' Say remembered getting on bikes with his friends and going to the fort after it was abandoned. Then he went into his back room and came out with a 50-caliber ammo box that he had found there. Say kept his farming tools inside the ammo box. I kidded him and said one of those tools looks like one I left behind in 1968. We had a good laugh. As we were leaving, Say told us, 'Next time you come back, you stay at our house!' "

Before the Muths left Vietnam, their guide took them to Vung Tau Beach, where Dick had landed in January 1967 on the USS Geiger.

"I remember in 1967 we got off the ship by climbing down the cargo ropes. We went to a place we called Newport, over on the Saigon River, north of Saigon. We hauled a lot of equipment from Newport to various Army units. On our return trip last year, our guide took us to Tay

Ninh City and down to Cu Chi, where we learned that the old base camp was also still in use by the Vietnamese military, just like French Fort."

After 49 years of married life, Darlene Muth is happy to have visited the country that had such an impact on her husband when he was just a young man.

"I was filled with trepidation on the plane ride to Vietnam," Darlene wrote in a Facebook post, "but I am so thankful I experienced this with Dick. (Say's) family was very personable and even invited us to stay with them the next time we go to Vietnam."

Dick Muth came home from Vietnam on Jan. 6, 1968. Like a lot of Vietnam vets, Dick always wondered what happened after he left the war zone. His return trip in 2018 filled in some details. But a real revelation came in early 2019 when Dick read a book about the artillery unit that occupied Camp Saint Barbara (aka French Fort) from 1968 until near the end of the war. Muth made connections with the 2nd Battalion, 32nd Field Artillery through its website and Facebook page. He posted some photos that elicited memories from a group of veterans who had served at French Fort with A Battery, 2/32 artillery.

As Dick learned, the old fort became a very dangerous place by the summer of 1968 when the North Vietnamese Army brass decided all of this intersecting artillery fire was crippling their plans to create mayhem in Tay Ninh Province. The enemy began planting land mines almost nightly on the only road to Camp Saint Barbara. That road was important to the everyday lives of the soldiers inside the camp. Food and laundry arrived by truck. Artillery shells and other forms of weapons and ammunition were resupplied over the road. Replacement soldiers often came by truck. Five of them died in a land mine explosion on June 12, 1968. Three more American troops died on Aug. 23. After another explosion killed two soldiers on Sept. 2, the road was closed down for several months. The only resupply would come via helicopter or plane.

Camp Saint Barbara underwent 42 straight days of mortar and rocket attacks from early August until Sept. 17,1968 when a direct hit outside the FDC bunker killed two infantry officers and took the legs from A Battery commander Donald Babb. Captain Babb, a West Point graduate, had arrived in his new post in early August and immediately realized the camp needed additional fortification. He talked the battalion commander into installing a 105-mm artillery gun and crew at the front gate, along with infantry support. The front gate, Babb realized, was "wide open." In a night attack, the enemy could have moved right up that road, past the garbage dump, and within yards of the fort's berm.

This additional protection eventually dissuaded enemy intentions to attack the fort. Nobody was going to overrun Camp Saint Barbara although a sapper squad attack in August 1969 killed two artillery soldiers. A Battery would remain at the camp for the next two years, sometimes sending gun platoons on missions over near the Cambodian border. The II Field Force command would eventually build smaller FSBs even closer to Cambodia, bases with names like Illingworth, Jay, Pace, Beverly and Carolyn. During the months preceding the June 1970 Cambodian "incursion," these smaller bases would serve as "bait," luring the enemy out of the jungle on the other side of the border. A platoon of A Battery soldiers fought side by side with infantry at The Battle of Illingworth on April 1, 1970, losing three soldiers while the infantry lost 21 in a hand-to-hand fight to the death. Only when the enemy blew up a stockpile of artillery shells did the fighting end, in an explosion that catapulted soldiers into the air and temporarily disabled their ear drums.

Camp Saint Barbara would remain standing until the end of the war. One can only surmise that the North Vietnamese used American bases as holding places for the South Vietnamese "traitors" who were arrested at the war ended in April 1975. And once the country stabilized under communist forces, those American outposts were scavenged for salvageable equipment. The jungle would eventually overtake them, reclaiming the land and returning it to its natural state.

Dick Muth got to see all that, got to see how Vietnam countryside had changed over the past 50 years. His questions had been answered, and Darlene was beside him to witness this conclusion of a long journey.

Muth was asked what advice he would offer any Vietnam veterans still interested in seeing the place they had visited and fought for with their lives many years before.

"I would tell them to go with an open mind. You will be treated very fairly," he said. "The country has developed over the years. Saigon is a first-class city. We stayed at the Grand Hotel, which is so nice, it would fit right into Manhattan. I would tell them to try and find the place where they were stationed. Most of it has changed but we could still see the piers at Newport harbor, and the bridge across the river that the Americans had built. We went back to Bien Hoa Air Base and looked through the fence. Long Binh base camp is now an industrial park. It looks nothing like it did during the war.

"I would caution returning veterans about the War Museum in Saigon. It's very controversial. There is a lot of information slanted against the United States, especially about our bombing of the north and the effects of Agent Orange on their population. When we went to the museum, our guide warned us that the Agent Orange display is very disturbing. The Cu Chi Tunnel Museum was also difficult because they had piles of old weapons, rocket and grenade launchers, an old shot-up helicopter, a couple of APCs and a tank, all of them pretty shot up. The museums were pretty slanted against the Americans."

Dick and Darlene Muth returned home on that long flight across the Pacific with a greater understanding of Vietnam, past and present. The old soldier is at peace now with his memories.

OLD FRIENDS – A group of veterans from Pennsbury High's Class of 1965 participated in a luncheon on the day of their 50th reunion. (Photo courtesy of Kathy Hull Ross)

EPILOGUE
We All Love America

BY TERRY NAU

Whenever I am around people of my generation, the Baby Boomers, one thing that always shines through is how much we love our country. Friends share notes on vacation trips they have made over the years, to all parts of America. We seem to have been inspired by the beauty of our national parks. We have driven through the cornfields of Iowa and the dairy farms of Wisconsin. As we have grown older, everywhere in the USA looks pretty nice.

More importantly, the Baby Boomers co-exist peacefully in their golden years, sharing a mutual love of America and the precious nature of life.

It was not always this way. After we left high school in the mid-1960s, many different forces began to pull our generation apart. The war in Southeast Asia instigated almost all of these pressures. Friends who went off to college came under the influence of professors who disagreed with expanding the war in Vietnam. Anti-war activists even questioned the morality of the United States' intentions in Vietnam! Us. America. The country that saved the world only 20 years earlier. Our parents were naturally upset with the divisions growing in the generation that followed theirs.

Others from my Pennsylvania hometown went to work in the local steel mill, listening to their parents and co-workers who believed in their country, right or wrong. And then there were the teenagers who joined the military right away, guys like Jimmy Grauel and Terry Wallace whose stories were told in this book. Jimmy wanted to get away from home. Terry weighed his options and decided to bank on the draft, only to find himself assigned to the Marine Corps. There was also an

227

element of fearlessness among people who would make that kind of decision, to join the military with a war busting out in Southeast Asia. They must have been looking for some excitement. Some, like David Christian, wanted to use the Army as their ticket to a college education they otherwise could not afford without the help of the G.I. Bill.

Let's not forget the people who wanted no part of the war but would report for duty when the draft board came calling. We were not heroes. Thank you for your service? I hear that a lot nowadays but I didn't volunteer to serve. I got drafted into the Army. A majority of us who served were drafted. And many of us did use the G.I. Bill to get our college educations, after we came home.

Those of us who did go into the military quickly learned how bad things were elsewhere in the world. It only took a few days in Vietnam before we began longing for the luxuries taken for granted while growing up. Like grocery stores, with real food. Pizza. Ice cream. Cars and girls, music on the radio.

No matter where the military took us, we soon realized how people in other countries often struggled to survive. The great shock of entering Vietnam, after the initial assault on the senses created by oppressive heat and dirt and the smell of diesel fuel, was the abject poverty we saw in those first few days, as we were driven in trucks to our unit, passing through small villages comprised of mud huts and very little concrete. Little children running around naked. Adults wearing the same flimsy clothes every day. Water buffalo strolling through the village, waiting to go to work in the rice paddies. It was a world with which we were not familiar.

While our college friends pushed ahead with their education, expanding their own horizons, soldiers in Vietnam often battled rats for sleeping space. They slept on air mattresses, bathing in their own sweat. While our college friends went to football games and partied on weekends, we laid low during mortar attacks. Infantry soldiers like Jimmy Grauel and Don Bentivoglio went out on patrols in the jungle, risking their lives for an increasingly murky objective. We didn't make the connection while fighting the war but when we returned home, there was a definite sense that civilians did not appreciate all the things we take for granted in America.

It's no wonder we had little to talk about with our friends when we came home from what Terry Wallace fittingly called "The Suck" in his chapter of this book. What did we have in common? So there began this long period of awkward friendships where people on both sides did not know how to talk to each other. Vietnam veterans did not want to share. People who did not serve in the military at all were hesitant to ask what it was like to work for Uncle Sam. Veterans who did not get posted to Vietnam felt guilty, too, as Jim Raftus points out in his chapter. They did not need to feel guilty but we were all victims of strange feelings in those days.

When did the hard feelings among war veterans begin to break down? My guess is the First Gulf War in 1991. That's when the Army, led by Vietnam veterans like Colin Powell, made plans to bring soldiers home to a warm welcome. Soldiers would not come home alone anymore, as they had during the Vietnam War. One Army post in North Carolina invited area Vietnam veterans to welcome home the troops from Iraq. Perhaps this is where the awkward silence began to melt away.

As our 50th high school reunion approached, my circle of childhood friends had become comfortable with each other again. Vietnam veterans had "come out of the closet," as one Army psychologist told me, and were easier to engage about the war, as long as the questions were not specific, or obnoxious. We held a Veterans' Luncheon at the reunion of Pennsbury High's Class of 1965. Some of the women from our class stood in the back of the room and watched as we honored two classmates who were killed in Vietnam. We all had something in common now, a general sadness over what we had lost in the 1960s. We lost friends, and acquired a cynicism that was hard to shake.

I first started to hear the voices of Vietnam in my head back in 2003 when a few members of my artillery unit met in Las Vegas for our first reunion, 35 years after we had departed the war zone. This is where the dialogue began for me, after so many years of silence. We told old stories, embellishing them wherever possible, laughing together over some incidents that were not all that funny back in 1967 or 1968 when we were riding around Tay Ninh province, shooting fire missions and supporting our infantry brothers whenever possible.

229

Back home, among family and friends, there had never been much dialogue about the war. Which was fine. Only about one in 10 of us actually got sent to Vietnam. So it was awkward to hear that occasional question ... what was it really like over there? Messed up was a sufficient answer. Those two words steered the conversation on to another subject.

Turns out the only people whose voices I wanted to hear again were those guys from my old unit.

After I retired in 2012, the voices grew louder. Work was no longer interfering with my day. There was more time to look back. It's no secret, the Vietnam War really did split the Baby Boomer Generation back in the 1960s. There was no running from the war. It caught all of us in one way or another. And when it was over, most of us just stashed the war away and went on with our lives.

That burial of a bad memory is most commonly associated with Vietnam War veterans but my sense is that everyone tried to forget about the war. The anti-war protestors shared with us one common goal – let's forget about the war. Vietnam was just a bad time for our country, and President Nixon's problems with the Watergate break-in only exacerbated our feelings. Watergate and Vietnam bewildered so many of us, and turned us into cynics.

Five decades later, a new appreciation of Vietnam has settled into our country's soul. It appears in different places. During my annual visit in June 2019 to the Veterans Administration for a physical checkup, my doctor told me he served during the First Gulf War.

"You Vietnam veterans paved the way for Gulf War veterans," the doctor said, "because for so long, the government did not recognize the effects of Agent Orange. When they finally did, it was because the Vietnam vets fought for it. They opened the door for Gulf War veterans who had been exposed to poisonous chemicals in Iraq and Kuwait."

That reminded me of the strongest voice of the Vietnam War I have encountered – David Christian, the combat hero who came home and began advocating for veterans from his bed at Valley Forge Military Hospital. Dave is a Republican who twice ran for a Congressional seat in Bucks County during the 1980s. During our interview for this

230

book, I asked Dave how he felt about the anti-war protestors, half-expecting a rant against those who marched in the streets, and sometimes belittled our soldiers. Instead, Dave spoke rationally about what makes this country great – free speech.

"I respect the anti-war protestors for standing up for their cause," he said. "That is what America is all about."

Christian went on to lament the lack of decisiveness among our nation's leaders, a point his fellow war veterans and anti-war protestors could both appreciate.

"The problem we had was the politicians could not agree on how to fight the Vietnam War. They couldn't make a decision. We needed politicians who would make a stand on the war. As a soldier, I would have been proud of a government leader who acted decisively on Vietnam," he said.

David Christian had one more thought on the Vietnam War.

"I recall listening to a General from India who was speaking at a 50-year remembrance ceremony for the war. He asked: 'Why do people say Vietnam veterans are losers? You Vietnam veterans completed your mission. You stopped communism.'

"Every Vietnam veteran says that we were winning when they left Vietnam," Christian added. "The war may have been lost in Washington or Saigon but Vietnam veterans were successful in their mission – communism never spread past the borders of Vietnam. Thailand, Cambodia and India were all free of communism because of the sacrifices of Vietnam veterans."

David Christian's point is an important message for Vietnam veterans to hear, even if the exact details remain foggy to this day. His words tell American veterans that those 58,000-plus soldiers did not die in vain. That is what we grasp for in our golden years. We all take great pride that we answered the call back when we were young. Nobody can take that away from us. We want to think our heroes died for a cause, even if it was just to save the soldier next to them. We do know that communism died in most of the world in the late 1980s when the Berlin Wall came down.

The voices of the Vietnam War today have changed in tone, in part because 50 years is a long time to hold a grudge. We have all mellowed. There is a respect for soldiers now, and for veterans, that some members of our generation lost sight of in the 1960s. Those who protested the war still believe in their hearts they did the right thing, perhaps regretting only the anger that was directed at war veterans after they came home from Vietnam. As Steve Walach hints in his chapter, maybe the protestors did not present their message properly. Maybe they were too strident and not respectful enough of the Greatest Generation.

What seems true is we have a mutual respect on both sides now that was missing during the heated days of our youth. Veterans went to war and learned something important about themselves. Protestors fought their own fight at home and remained true to their principles. We are the survivors of that hectic time in our lives.

ABOUT THE AUTHOR

Terry Nau graduated from Pennsbury High School in 1965. Drafted into the Army a year later, Nau served as an artillery specialist in the Vietnam War from September 1967 until late August 1968.

Returning home, Nau enrolled at the Pennsylvania State University and graduated with a degree in communications four years later, in March 1972. After spending 40 years in the newspaper business as a sports writer and editor, Nau retired in 2012. The only thing he missed about work was the writing. And so it became the Vietnam War that filled the void. Writing about people he knew, and soldiers who died, Nau self-published five books on the war. This one, *Voices of the Vietnam War*, should be his last!

IN HIS OWN VOICE – Terry Nau found time in retirement to reflect on the Vietnam War. (Photo by Cheryl Britland)

Made in the USA
Monee, IL
06 November 2019